The
MA & PA

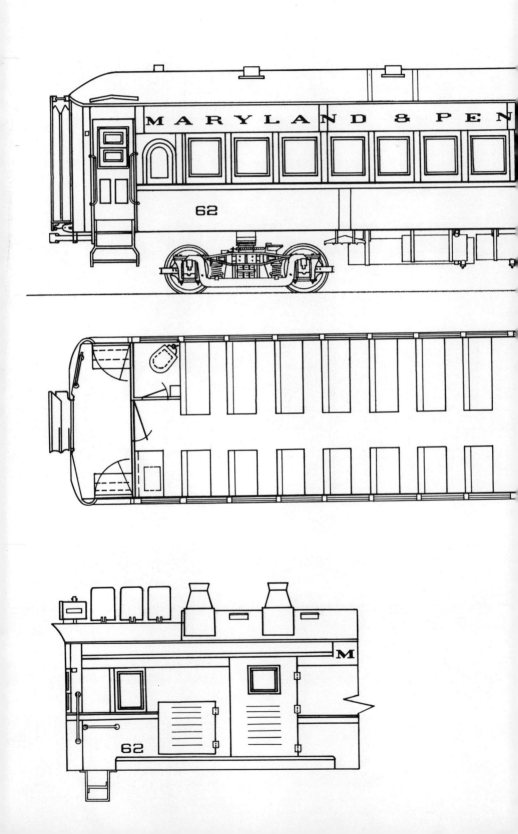

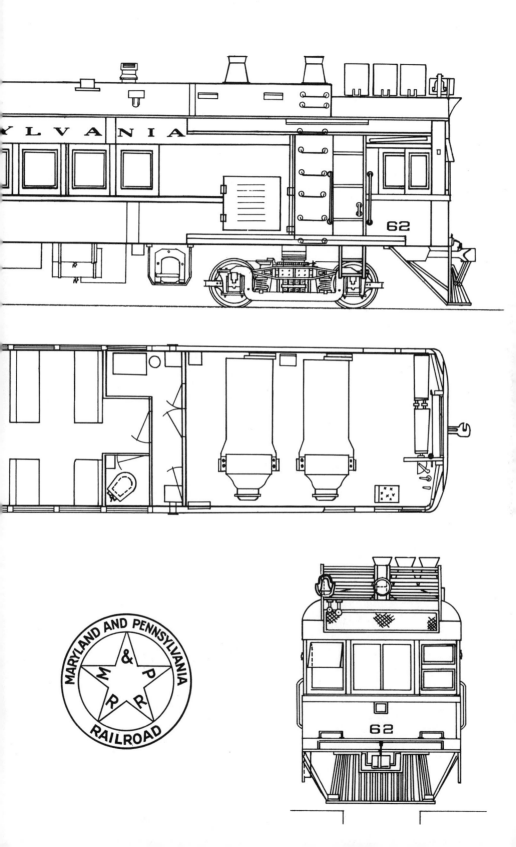

By the same author:

Cable Railways of Chicago

The Electric Interurban Railways in America (in collaboration with John F. Due)

The Truck System

The Great Lakes Car Ferries

The Toledo, Port Clinton & Lakeside Railway

The Staten Island Ferry

The Night Boat

The Transportation Act of 1958

The Cable Car in America

Federal Transit Subsidies

The Northeast Railroad Problem

The Illustrated History of Paddle Steamers (in collaboration with Joseph Jobe and Russell Plummer)

Monon Route

Amtrak

American Narrow Gauge Railroads

Eastland: Legacy of the Titanic

Nellie Farren

Edited works:

A Treatise upon Cable or Rope Traction as Applied to the Working of Street and Other Railways (1887) by J. Bucknall Smith

The Annotated Baseball Stories of Ring W. Lardner, 1914–1919

The Front Page by Ben Hecht and Charles MacArthur

The

MA & PA

A History of THE MARYLAND & PENNSYLVANIA RAILROAD

Second Edition, Revised

By George W. Hilton

The Johns Hopkins University Press
Baltimore and London

Printed in the United States of America on acid-free paper

Johns Hopkins Paperbacks edition, 1999
9 8 7 6 5 4 3 2 1

The Johns Hopkins University Press
2715 North Charles Street
Baltimore, Maryland 21218-4363
www.press.jhu.edu

Library of Congress Cataloging-in-Publication Data

Hilton, George Woodman.
   The ma & pa : a history of the Maryland & Pennsylvania
Railroad / by George W. Hilton. — 2nd ed., rev.
      p.   cm.
   Originally published : Howell-North Books, c1980.
   Includes index.
   ISBN 0-8018-6294-9 (pbk. : alk. paper)
   1. Maryland and Pennsylvania Railroad—History.   I. Title.
HE2791.M3563H54   1999
385´.06´5752—dc21   99-32830

A catalog record for this book is available from the British Library.

To
the Men and Women of
the Maryland & Pennsylvania Railroad

Preface, 1999

It is, of course, gratifying to have a work of enthusiasm written in one's thirties republished by a university press in one's seventies. As readers seem not generally to realize, an author's esteem for his book tends to fall as time passes. An author thinks of changes he might have made or additions he might have undertaken. At worst, such feelings reach neurotic levels in which the author repudiates the book and seeks to buy up the existing stock for destruction. On a normal level, such feelings keep authors humble, or at least should do so.

In this instance, my principal retrospective evaluation is that I failed to recognize the generality of the experience I was describing. I had been aware that the Maryland & Pennsylvania had excessive curves and choppy grades, but it was not until I wrote this book that I realized how bad the problem was for the railroad. In writing my *American Narrow Gauge Railroads* (Stanford, Calif., 1990) I came to recognize how nearly universal the situation was among narrow gauge railroads and their standard gauge successors.

Another major problem described in this book, the incentive to convert to standard gauge in the 1890s, combined with the difficulty of financing conversion during the depression of the time, also proved to be more general than I realized. Most importantly, the narrow gauge predecessors of the Maryland & Pennsylvania perfectly demonstrated the technological problem that was the immediate cause of the narrow gauge movement's demise. The weight of locomotives tended to increase steadily throughout the history of the movement, essentially amounting to a path of convergence to standard gauge practice. Narrow gauges adopted heavier rails and otherwise sought to adapt their physical plants, but it was too costly to replace their bridges and trestles. Narrow gauge construction standards had entailed too many trestles, in any case. The consequence was that trestle collapse became the most characteristic form of accident on narrow gauge railroads. When I sought to document the weight escalation of narrow gauge locomotives for *American Narrow Gauge Railroads,* I could find no better quantification than in the rosters in the final pages of the book at hand. If I noticed this escalation when assembling the roster, it made no particular impression on me. Inevitably, the book documents some representative trestle collapses, or near misses. I should have shown the readers that this book is a more general treatise on the practice and problems of narrow gauge railroading than I did.

The original publisher of the book, the late Morgan North, counseled his authors to be satisfied with their books in what he knew would be the downward path of their evaluations. He died over twenty years ago, and his firm is long gone, but I have no doubt he would take pride in *The Ma & Pa,* a book he particularly enjoyed, having found a home in its later years with the Johns Hopkins University Press.

Preface

Like many of its admirers, I discovered the Maryland & Pennsylvania Railroad through an excellent article in *Trains* of December 1941 by William M. Moedinger, Jr. On the basis of Moedinger's careful description, I concluded that the Ma & Pa was a gem among gems, and I swore to visit the line at the earliest opportunity. That, as it proved, was none too early, for I was unable to make the pilgrimage until my last trip home from college in 1946. Even then I saw only the York terminal, which was, however, a pretty good sample of the company's archaic charms.

In 1949 I had my first academic appointment at the University of Maryland. Although it is entirely untrue that I chose this post for proximity to the Ma & Pa, the fact remains that one of the pleasures of the position was the opportunity to visit the line occasionally. I found it all that Moedinger's article had led me to expect: graceful antique equipment, marvelous scenery, formidable operating problems, and an over-all charm that would have been difficult to equal on any railroad. Admittedly, there is no Mount Robson on the Ma & Pa, the Muddy Creek valley is not the Feather River canyon, and the grades up to Red Lion are not to be compared with Raton Pass. On the other hand, much of western scenery is, to my taste, too bleak to be beautiful. If one fancies the wooded mountains of the East, and rolling hill country, the Ma & Pa offers a beauty hard to match.

It is little wonder that the Ma & Pa has a legion of enthusiasts. Fortunately, I was able to draw on many of them for assistance in preparing this book. In particular, I had access to two superb collections, one in Pennsylvania and the other in Maryland. William Moedinger, who had cultivated my interest in the first place, assisted me with information and photographs from his large collection at Lancaster. Similarly, Charles T. Mahan, Jr., of Baltimore, permitted me to draw on his collection, gathered over the course of some 25 years of interest in the Ma & Pa. Both these men were excellent photographers, who united technical competence with a feel for the atmosphere of the Ma & Pa. Toward the end of my researches I encountered Benjamin F. G. Kline, Jr., of Lancaster, who is preparing a history of the Lancaster Oxford & Southern. He was a great help to me in my short chapter on that unfortunate railroad. I am indebted to many others whose names appear in the photo captions and the notes to the roster.

Original cartography is by James A. Bier of the Department of Geography of the University of Illinois.

One of my greatest debts is to the late Charles B. Chaney, who tirelessly gathered material on the Maryland & Pennsylvania and other eastern railroads throughout a long life. After his death in 1948, his vast collection of roster data, photographs, and meticulous engine drawings was deposited in the Smithsonian Institution, where all may draw upon it. John H. White, Curator of Land Transportation at the Smithsonian, was extremely helpful in making the Chaney material available to me.

Not the least of my obligations is to the Maryland & Pennsylvania Railroad itself, which unstintingly provided me with information, and made available photographs from its historical collection. The contrast is striking between the helpfulness of this small company in really desperate financial straits, and a few large railroads which will answer no historical enquiries.

Like most scholars, I strive to be definitive in my writing. In this instance, however, I am quite content that the book contains a glaring omission: material on the ultimate abandonment of the railroad. I should guess the odds are worse than even that within a decade someone will record the date of the last trip and the details of the dismantling operation. I am thoroughly pleased that this history is published with the Maryland & Pennsylvania yet a going concern, and that, consequently, I can end my book with a hope that the railroad may long continue, rather than with a farewell salute to its past glories.

Contents

Chronology of Major Events

1867	Maryland Central Railroad chartered.
1868	Peach Bottom Railway chartered.
July 4, 1874	Peach Bottom Ry. opened York-Red Lion.
April, 1876	Baltimore Towsontown Dulaney's Valley & Delta Narrow Gauge Railway organized.
1878	Baltimore Towsontown Dulaney's Valley & Delta merged with Baltimore Hampden & Towsontown Railway to form Baltimore & Delta Railway.
1881	Peach Bottom Ry. goes bankrupt.
March 17, 1882	York & Peach Bottom Railway succeeds Peach Bottom Ry.
April 17, 1882	Baltimore & Delta Ry. opened from Baltimore to Towsontown.
August 28, 1882	Baltimore & Delta Ry. merged into Maryland Central R.R.
March, 1883	York & Peach Bottom Ry. extended to Peach Bottom.
June 21, 1883	Maryland Central RR reaches Bel Air.
January 21, 1884	Maryland Central reaches Delta.
October, 1884	Maryland Central RR goes bankrupt.
December 10, 1888	Maryland Central Railway succeeds Maryland Central R.R.
January, 1889	Maryland Central Ry. leases York & Peach Bottom Ry.
May 5, 1891	Maryland Central Ry. and York & Peach Bottom Ry. merged to form Baltimore & Lehigh Railroad.

December, 1892	Baltimore Forwarding & Railroad Company assumes property for conversion to standard gauge.
1893	Baltimore & Lehigh RR goes bankrupt.
1894	W. F. Walworth organizes York Southern Railroad to operate Pennsylvania mileage and J. W. Brown organizes Baltimore & Lehigh Railway to operate Maryland trackage.
1895	York Southern converts York-Delta mileage to 4'-8½".
1898	York Southern converts Peach Bottom branch to 4'-8½".
May 20, 1899	Dallastown branch opened.
August 23, 1900	Baltimore & Lehigh Ry. converts Baltimore-Delta to 4'-8½".
February 12, 1901	Baltimore & Lehigh Ry. and York Southern RR merged to form Maryland & Pennsylvania Railroad.
September 1, 1903	Peach Bottom branch abandoned.
December 28, 1917	United States Railroad Administration takes over M&PA.
June 29, 1918	M&PA returned to private management.
November, 1946	M&PA orders first Diesel locomotives.
May 4, 1947	Sunday passenger service discontinued.
October 1, 1951	Passenger service reduced to one train per day.
May, 1954	York-Baltimore through freights discontinued.
August 31, 1954	Passenger service discontinued.
November 29, 1956	End of steam operation.
June 11, 1958	Maryland District abandoned.
October 15, 1959	M&PA applies for complete abandonment; application refused by ICC in 1960.
March 31, 1969	Restoration of Peach Bottom branch.
October 4, 1971	Control of M&PA acquired by Emons Industries.
April 1, 1976	M&PA extended to Hyde, PA, and Walkersville, MD.
March 31, 1978	Walkersville line cut back to Littlestown.
June 14, 1978	M&PA embargoes main line beyond Red Lion.

The
MA & PA

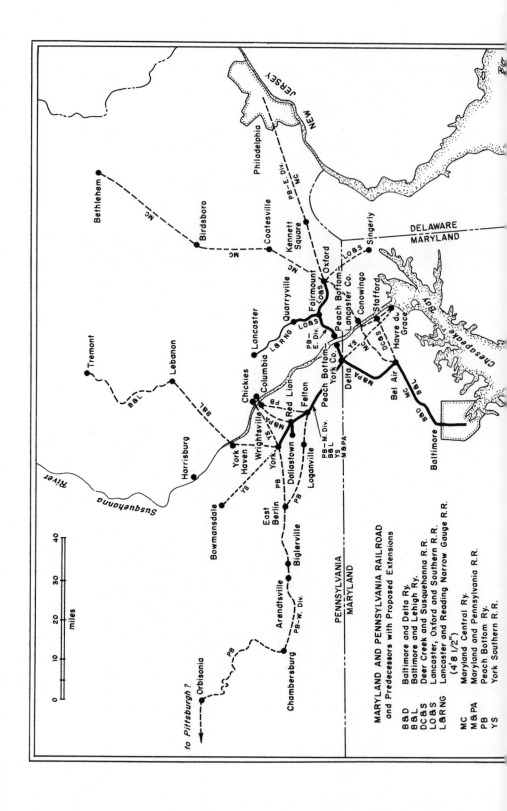

MARYLAND AND PENNSYLVANIA RAILROAD
and Predecessors with Proposed Extensions

B&D   Baltimore and Delta Ry.
B&L   Baltimore and Lehigh Ry.
DC&S   Deer Creek and Susquehanna R.R.
LO&S   Lancaster, Oxford and Southern R.R.
L&RNG Lancaster and Reading Narrow Gauge R.R.
          (4' 8 1/2")

MC   Maryland Central Ry.
M&PA Maryland and Pennsylvania R.R.
PB   Peach Bottom Ry.
YS   York Southern R.R.

1

The Peach Bottom Railway

THOSE WHO RODE the Maryland & Pennsylvania Railroad will not be surprised to learn that the line was not conceived as a direct route from Baltimore to York. Indeed, many who rode the Ma & Pa doubtless concluded that it was not designed to be a direct route anywhere, and that the whole railroad was simply created as a work of art. After all, the road connected two cities some 49 miles apart with a rail line of 77.2 miles rambling through the loveliest of the Maryland hill country, and following a marvelously beautiful river valley for most of its mileage in Pennsylvania. The motive power would have done credit to any good museum of antique technology, and the rolling stock had a consistency and originality that might well have come from the hand of a great artist. Any of the hundreds of visitors who came to see the Ma & Pa between 1935 and 1954 might easily have concluded that the whole thing came from the mind of some Velásquez or Rembrandt among model railroaders, who, having exhausted his art in HO and O gauges, came finally to the hills north of Baltimore to create his masterpiece at a scale of 12 inches to the foot.

Whatever may be the superficial attractions of such an interpretation, the cold light of history reveals that the Maryland & Pennsylvania was conceived in the same hope of pecuniary gain as less picturesque enterprises. The hundreds upon hundreds of curves in its right-of-way testified only to its narrow gauge ancestry, and the antique quality of its later years was the product of a genteel poverty. The right angle in its right-of-way at the Mason-Dixon Line indicated that the railroad had been built by two predecessor companies, designed for divergent purposes,

S. G. Boyd

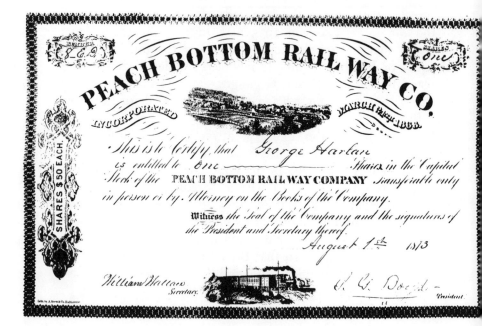

united only by their frustration at reaching their goals, and by an interest in hauling slate out of the quarries at Delta, Pennsylvania.

Of the Ma & Pa's two narrow gauge predecessors, the earlier, the more prosperous, and, as it proved, the longer lasting, was the northern. The line from York to Delta was built in the 1870's by the Peach Bottom Railway Company as part of a grandiose scheme for a line across the southern tier of Pennsylvania from Philadelphia to the Broad Top coal fields, or possibly even on to Pittsburgh. Such a line would have been a major rival to the Pennsylvania Railroad, which was looked upon locally as something of a monopoly. The projected railway might easily have found a more promising route than the tortuous passage up Muddy Creek gorge in York County (for example, the present route of the Pennsylvania Turnpike, graded by Vanderbilt's South Penn Railway), but the Peach Bottom was a local enterprise, promoted mainly by York County people who were incidentally intent upon improving local service in their area. There had been ferry service across the Susquehanna River between two towns named Peach Bottom, one in York County and the other in Lancaster County, since about 1725, and by the 1870's, there were two ferry lines connecting the two Peach Bottoms. The route from York County to Philadelphia via Peach Bottom was, admittedly, a minor one, but it did have an appreciable traffic, and it was not outlandish to promote a railroad along it.

The railroad was to be in three parts. The first, the Eastern Division, was to run from Peach Bottom, Lancaster County, to Oxford, and then, probably through Lincoln and Kennett Square to Philadelphia. The second, the Middle Division, was to be built from Peach Bottom, York County, to Delta, up Muddy Creek to Felton, and then west to Hanover Junction, York, or some other point, where it would connect with the line west. This, the Western Division, was the most nebulous of the lot. It was intended to run on some ill-defined route through the country north of Gettysburg, then hurdle the formidable mountains to the west, and come to rest around Orbisonia in the coal fields. There was assuredly plenty of eastbound coal traffic to syphon off the Pennsylvania, and thus the projected road had considerable plausibility, provided only that some way could be found to cross the mountains and to bridge the Susquehanna. Those provisos were not to be taken lightly, and were, in fact, enough to frustrate the entire project. Before the ultimate collapse of the Peach Bottom System, however, enough track had been laid to create the northern portion of the Ma & Pa and a 20-mile narrow gauge on the east side of the Susquehanna, the Lancaster Oxford & Southern.

The Peach Bottom Railway took shape in the minds of its promoters in the middle 1860's. The principal figure in the project, and the man who is, more than any other, the founder of the Ma & Pa, was Stephen G. Boyd. He had been born at Peach Bottom, York County, in 1830, and had been trained as a teacher. He held a degree from Millersville State Normal School, and in 1852 he began a career of teaching that lasted 14 years. At the end of the Civil War he was principal of the school at Wrightsville. In 1866 he was elected to the Pennsylvania state legislature as a Democrat, representing York County. On March 24, 1868, he drafted and secured passage of a bill incorporating the Peach Bottom Railway Company. Nothing was done immediately to implement the incorporation, but in 1871 the railroad was organized with Boyd as President. Samuel R. Dickey of Oxford was Vice-President, and the directors were an equitable mixture of businessmen from York, Lancaster and Chester counties. Significantly, no one from the western reaches of the proposed line was represented in the new company.

The Peach Bottom Railway set out in the orthodox fashion to secure stock subscriptions, and by December 1, 1871, had enough to justify beginning to survey its route. As chief engineer, the road hired Colonel John M. Hood, a Union army veteran of considerable engineering talent, who was later to earn prominence as president of the Western Maryland Railway. Hood, upon traversing the Muddy Creek valley, reported to the directors at Peach Bottom, strongly recommending building the railroad with 3'-0" gauge. He recognized that the road would be a continual series of curves, and argued, in the same fashion as engineers in Colorado, that narrow gauge would permit sharper curves and let the management get away with lower investment in the bargain. The directors accepted Hood's logic and decided that the road should be narrow gauge. It hardly need be said that this was a disastrous error, one which beset the Ma & Pa with operating problems that plague it to this day. The directors, at least, had plenty of com-

TRAINS GOING WEST.

STATIONS.	No. 1. A. M.	No. 2. P. M.
Leave Woodbine	7.15	3.45
" Bridgetown	7.20	3.49
" Bruce	7.25	3.55
" Muddy Creek Forks	7.35	4.05
" High Rock	7.40	4 10
" Laurel	7.50	4.20
" Fenmore	7.57	4.30
" Felton	8.05	4.40
" Windsor	8.10	4.45
" Springvale	8.18	4.53
" Red Lion	8.25	5.00
" Dallastown	8.35	5.15
" Ore Valley	8.40	5.23
" Enterprize	8 45	5.30
" Small's Mill	8 54	5.39
" Spring Garden	9.00	5.45
Arrive York	9.00	5.45

TRAINS GOING EAST.

STATIONS.	No. 1. P. M.	No. 2. P. M.
Leave York	1 30	7.00
" Spring Garden	1.32	7.02
" Small's Mill	1.36	7.06
" Enterprize	1.45	7.15
" Ore Valley	1 52	7.20
" Dallastown	2 00	7.25
" Red Lion	2 15	7.35
" Springvale	2 22	7.42
" Windsor	2.30	7.50
" Felton	2.35	7 55
" Fenmore	2 45	8 03
" Laurel	2.55	8.10
" High Rock	3.05	8.20
" Muddy Creek Forks	3 10	8.25
" Bruce	3.20	8.35
" Bridgetown	3.20	8.40
Arrive Woodbine	3 30	8.45

No. 1 train, west, connects with N. C. R. W. with train arriving in Baltimore at 1.10 P. M.

No. 1 train, east, connects with N. C. R. W. with train leaving Baltimore at 8.25 A. M., and with P. R. R. with train leaving Philadelphia at 8 A. M.

No. 2 train, east, connects with N. C. R. W. with train leaving Baltimore at 3.25 P. M.   S. G. BOYD, President.

pany, for the narrow gauge fever was just beginning, and several hundred other companies were to make the same mistake within the next few decades. If anything, one must be more lenient toward the Peach Bottom's directors than toward the builders of the later narrow gauges. Boyd and his associates had no precedent to guide them. The Denver & Rio Grande was just building the first important American narrow gauge, and it was not until the 1880's that the disadvantages were widely demonstrated. The Peach Bottom's directors in later years may have taken melancholy pleasure in being pioneers in error.

When Hood began his survey, the route west from the head of the Muddy Creek valley at Felton was not yet determined. As usual at the time, the promoters sounded out local prospects for financial assistance. By 1872 Boyd had serious misgivings that the road could execute its original plan without great financial assistance from some quarter—and his various feelers showed no such source in the vicinity. The direct route to the coal fields from Felton was straight west over Neff's Summit to Hanover Junction, but Boyd found little prospect of raising capital in that sparsely populated area. About a year before his death in 1899, Boyd revealed that he had gone to Philadelphia at this time to hold a secret conversation with Franklin B. Gowan, the President of the Reading. Boyd proposed that the Reading help the Peach Bottom in its westward building, in return for which the Peach Bottom would lay a branch to Wrightsville, across the Susquehanna from a connection with the Reading at Columbia. Boyd, who had discovered that the people of Delta were somewhat more interested in a line to Baltimore than in his railroad to some undetermined point north and west, also suggested a Delta-Baltimore line to Gowan. Gowan listened courteously to Boyd, but turned him down flatly.

The prospect of the Peach Bottom's building from Felton to Hanover Junction was unpopular in York, which would have been left some ten miles above the Peach Bottom's connection with the Northern Central (now the Baltimore-Harrisburg line of the Pennsylvania) near Loganville. Consequently, a committee of York businessmen, led by Michael B. Spahr and David E. Small, approached the Peach Bottom's directors in an effort to attract the line to York. This was little less than a godsend to the

Porter-Bell was solidly convinced that the 2-4-0 was more appropriate for narrow gauge roads than the 4-4-0. It sold the Peach Bottom's management on the idea to the extent that three of the line's first four engines were Porter 2-4-0's. Above is Peach Bottom-Middle Division No. 2. *(Thomas A. Norrell collection)*

The Middle Division's No. 3 was a hard-riding Mason bogie which saw only about two years of service. *(Benjamin F. G. Kline, Jr., collection)*

railway, since its most vital need was a connection with the Northern Central, wherever it might be made. York was a city of 11,003 which held the prospect of considerable local traffic. The directors responded that they would build to York for stock subscriptions of $75,000. Spahr and Small replied they thought $50,000 could be raised. Not surprisingly, the Peach Bottom's directors accepted forthwith, and all was in readiness for what was to be the first stage of the great Peach Bottom System.

The York subscription was promptly paid, and grading began on the line from York over Red Lion summit, down to Felton and through the Muddy Creek valley. Spahr and his associates apparently thought that the prospects for the whole scheme were poor, but considered the $50,000 well spent to secure a line to the Red Lion area, which was an important local center of cigar manufacture and of the furniture and woodworking industry.

The grading at the outset was done on the proceeds of the stock subscription, but in 1873 the company prepared for its first bond issue. Just as the bonds were about to be issued to the public in the fall of the year, Jay Cooke & Co., the Philadelphia bankers who were financing the Northern Pacific, failed, precipitating the Panic of 1873. The Peach Bottom's directors were understandably disturbed, and considered suspending grading. Zachariah K. Loucks, a director and President of the First National Bank of York, argued strongly against this course, and swung the Board to his views. He argued that the company's stock subscriptions were secure, and that the panic would spend itself shortly. In one respect, the panic worked to the benefit of the Peach Bottom: York banks, in an effort to increase their liquidity, withdrew extensive cash balances from Philadelphia banks, and consequently had abundant loanable funds, some of which shortly found their way to the Peach Bottom.

The Panic of 1873 did, however, help to kill the proposed Western Division. In February 1873 Colonel Hood had been sent out to survey a route to the coal fields. He found no feasible route on his first trip, but on his second he recommended a line from York to East Berlin, Biglerville, Arendtsville, Cole's Narrows, and along the Chambersburg-Gettysburg road over South Mountain. Hood's survey caused great interest in the area, particularly at East Berlin, where a $25,000 subscription was

» 8 «

offered. The Peach Bottom's directors had lost none of their eagerness to reach the Broad Top coal field, particularly since the narrow gauge East Broad Top Railroad was now being built. If the Peach Bottom could join with the East Broad Top at Orbisonia, the two could form a through route without a gauge difference from a small but productive coal field to important markets in eastern Pennsylvania. However seductive this prospect looked to the directors, the geographical hurdles remained enormous. Even if the Peach Bottom could surmount vast South Mountain to reach the Chambersburg area, some six separate summits lay ahead in the Tuscarora Mountains between Chambersburg and Orbisonia. The completed railroad would have been a veritable narrow gauge New York Ontario & Western, surmounting summit after summit to reach a target barely worth the effort. Between the Panic of 1873 and the innate limitations of the project, the Western Division died peacefully without a spade dug in the ground in its behalf.

Work proceeded, however, on the Middle Division. By the spring of 1874 the grade had been completed from York to Red Lion, Felton and Woodbine, some 27 miles. About two miles of grade had been made from Peach Bottom up to Scott's Run, leaving a gap of nine miles from Scott's Run through Delta to Woodbine. On April 27, 1874, the Peach Bottom contracted with James A. Schall of York for a thousand tons of 30-pound rail at $65 per ton, and about May 1, tracklaying began. Gus Boyd, the 16-year-old son of the president, drove the first spike at York. About this time, Colonel Hood resigned to join the Western Maryland. He was succeeded as chief engineer by John E. Matthews, who served for less than a year before being replaced by his assistant, S. M. Manifold.

Tracklaying continued fairly rapidly, considering the difficulty of the terrain. The firm of Conley & Eppley had contracted to lay track, and two men from Peach Bottom, John A. Barnett and William Ramsay, installed bridges and trestles. By June 30, 1874, the line was completed to a point near Yoe, where a station called Dallastown was established. The first passenger train ran July 4, 1874. The railway had bought its first locomotive, apparently an o-6-o, and named it RUFUS WILEY, after a director who had recently died. Porter-Bell & Company of Pittsburgh had built her

Not long after completion of the railroad, Peach Bottom No. 3 and a mixed train pause in front of the Delta station. Below, No. 4 crosses a bridge in the Muddy Creek valley. *(Both, W. R. Hicks collection)* The Peach Bottom painted drivers, domes and tender in claret and red, but left the cab natural walnut. Lettering was in gilt.

for $6000. A second engine, a 2-4-0, came from the same builder later in the year. No. 2 bore the name S. G. BOYD, but for reasons which are a minor historical mystery, she was always known as "SOOKEE".

The line was opened to Red Lion by August, to Felton by October, and to Muddy Creek Forks by Christmas, 1874. The company had pretty thoroughly impoverished itself in construction, and in 1875 it was forced to make a bond issue for the remainder of the grading and tracklaying. A public meeting in Woodbine in July 1875 raised much of the needed money. Partly because of financial difficulty and partly because of the engineering problem of carving out a line along Muddy Creek, progress was very slow in 1875, and by the end of the year track had been laid only to Bridgeton, five miles beyond Muddy Creek Forks and some eight miles short of Delta. Progress was rapid in the spring of 1876, and about April 15 the railway reached Delta. Slate had been mined there for about a century; thus the road's major source of traffic was at hand. The road had cost about $472,500, or $13,500 per mile. Almost all of this had been expended in construction, for the entire right-of-way had cost only some $6000 to $8000. Many farmers had donated land to the narrow gauge, and most of the line through Muddy Creek valley ran through uninhabited country where the land could be had free.

Meanwhile, the Eastern Division of the Peach Bottom System was also making progress. By the end of 1875 track had reached Eldora, about 14 miles from the Middle Division's railhead. Local farmers had taken most of the stock of the Eastern Division and were themselves doing the grading. The Eastern Division reached Peach Bottom, Lancaster County, in 1878.

The Middle Division, although it had no connection with the Eastern Division, was doing quite well. In 1875, even though not yet completed, the line carried 44,791 passengers and grossed $22,227. For a road with two locomotives, four passenger cars and 24 freight cars, the Peach Bottom was progressing nicely. In 1876, thanks to completion to Delta, the road grossed $37,071, an increase of about two-thirds. The year 1876 saw the arrival of the line's third locomotive, a 19-ton Mason bogie.

Upon completion of the railroad to Delta, the directors were confronted with the problem of pushing on to Peach Bottom.

The grade had now been completed, but laying track and otherwise fitting out the line would cost $45,000 to $50,000. Boyd and Loucks strongly opposed building the extension, arguing that the town of Peach Bottom could never generate enough traffic to make the line pay. They saw no prospect of crossing the Susquehanna to reach the Eastern Division, even though the operators of the Eastern Division were extremely eager for a connection. Finally, Boyd argued that the money for the extension would be better spent on locomotives and rolling stock for the finished line. Mainly because many of the other directors represented the town of Peach Bottom, Boyd and Loucks lost this controversy, and the company resolved to push on to the Susquehanna as soon as funds were available. As a consequence of this dispute, Boyd was not re-elected president in January 1877, but was replaced by Charles R. McConkey, the proprietor of a store and mill at Peach Bottom. S. M. Manifold became superintendent.

Boyd's departure as president of the Peach Bottom Railway does not remove him from the history of the Maryland & Pennsylvania. His investigations five years earlier had shown him that there was considerable interest in a railroad from the Delta area to Baltimore, and he became active in the promotion of the south-end predecessors of the Ma & Pa.

Although the Peach Bottom Railway after 1877 was solidly in the hands of directors favorable to extension to the Susquehanna, the company had enough financial trouble that nothing could be done immediately to build the line. The Middle Division had been completed with a bonded indebtedness of $323,600. Many of the bonds had been issued at substantial discounts in order to build the last few miles into Delta. By the spring of 1881 interest was in arrears on the Peach Bottom System's bonds, and creditors of both the Middle and Eastern Divisions sued for foreclosure. Both divisions were put in receivership in 1881. On September 1, the Eastern Division was sold for a modest $5000 to the trustees under the mortgage who organized the Peach Bottom Railroad. This line, the history of which is recounted in chapter III, thereafter pursued an independent course as a bucolic narrow gauge serving local farmers. It was never again affiliated with the Ma & Pa or its predecessors.

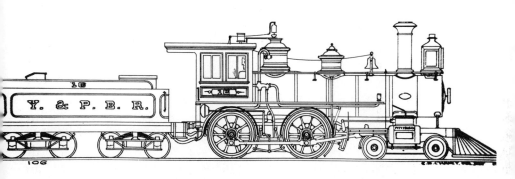

The York & Peach Bottom bought two Pittsburgh engines, No. 5, a 2-6-0, in 1882 and No. 6, a 4-4-0, in 1884. C. B. Chaney's drawings show them with the York & Peach Bottom's lettering, but with the numbers 15 and 16 they bore on the Baltimore & Lehigh. *(Smithsonian Institution; pass from Ward Kimball collection)*

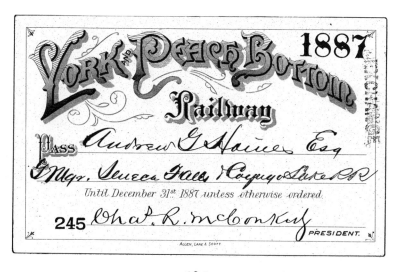

The Middle Division was sold to its bondholders on December 20, 1881. McConkey was able to remain in control of the line, and Manifold continued as operating head. On March 17, 1882, McConkey formed a new corporation, the York & Peach Bottom Railway Company. The name testified to McConkey's continuing eagerness to reach the Susquehanna now that the financial impediments to extension were out of the way. In June 1882 the company made arrangements for laying the 5.7 miles of track on what was now a long-completed grade. The line was opened about March 1883, approximately a year after the reorganization. Boyd considered his low opinion of the Peach Bottom extension thoroughly vindicated by experience. Near the end of the century he reported that the extension had never even paid its operating expenses. Since there was now no community of ownership with the narrow gauge on the eastern shore of the Susquehanna, the incentive to effect a crossing of the river had largely disappeared. There was little prospect of much through traffic developing now that the line to the coal fields was dead. As far as is known, the two narrow gauges connected only by means of the two ferry lines at Peach Bottom and by barge. All regular connection is believed to have been by break-bulk methods, and no car ferry is known to have operated.

Although the Peach Bottom extension did the company little good, the over-all showing of the line during the 1880's was satisfactory. In the fiscal year ending April 30, 1884, the York & Peach Bottom grossed $35,180 from freight, $20,565 from passengers, and $2,222 from head-end traffic. From its operations it made a net of $18,084, of which $12,520 was needed for interest payments. By 1889 the company was receiving feelers to combine with its southern connection, the Maryland Central, and then as now, there usually wasn't much eagerness to merge with unprosperous railroads.

2
The Maryland Central Railroad

THE EARLY HISTORY of the south-end predecessors of the Maryland & Pennsylvania is integral with a large number of projects to build a railroad from Baltimore to Philadelphia more or less along the route of the present U. S. Highway 1. For a project that was never executed, this proposal has a long history. Discussion began as early as the mid-1830's. The Baltimore & Susqehanna Company was chartered in 1836 to build from Baltimore to the river at Peach Bottom. The first important effort to build all the way from Philadelphia to Baltimore along this route dates from about 1858. The Philadelphia & Baltimore Central Railroad, the present Pennsylvania Railroad line from Philadelphia through Oxford and Lincoln to Port Deposit on the Susquehanna, was an effort to build such a line, but it foundered—like most of the Ma & Pa's dreams of glory—on an inability to bridge the river.

There were several projects to build a Baltimore-Philadelphia line via Bel Air in the 1860's. The Maryland Central Railroad was chartered to build such a line in 1867, intending to bridge the Susquehanna at Conowingo. It made no progress whatever in building the railroad, but it did secure a charter which included a very favorable financial provision: the City of Baltimore obligated itself to endorse the bonds of the company to the extent of $600,000 as soon as the company had spent $500,000 on the railroad. The municipal guaranty of the company's bonds would be a potent help in financing the railroad, if only the initial half-million could be raised and invested in the physical plant. The Maryland Central never raised the half-million, and by the 1870's it seemed to be just another of countless dead railroad projects. Events, as we shall see, were to bring it back to life in the 1880's.

In 1873 a prophetically named company, the Maryland & Pennsylvania Railroad, was organized to build generally along the route the Maryland Central had envisioned. L. Montgomery Bond of Philadelphia and Job Haines of Baltimore were its organizers, and its chief engineer was John M. Hood, whom we have previously encountered laying out the Peach Bottom Railway in Pennsylvania. The Maryland & Pennsylvania managed to get as far as grading, laying out about ten miles of right-of-way from a junction with the Northern Central at Relay House through Towsontown and a short distance to the east. A subsidiary incorporated in Pennsylvania, the Baltimore Philadelphia & New York Railroad, did a little grading in the vicinity of the Wilmington & Northern line south of West Chester.

The first Maryland & Pennsylvania was a quick and utter failure. Both the Maryland corporation and its Pennsylvania subsidiary went bankrupt in 1874. Although over $100,000 was said to have been spent on the project, both portions of the line were sold at sheriffs' sales for small sums. Walter Scott, the contractor who had graded the three miles from Relay House to Towsontown, bought the Maryland & Pennsylvania in 1877 for $1524. He intended to complete the line to Towsontown, but never did so. In 1878, the Baltimore Philadelphia & New York was sold to the Wilmington & Northern for $75. The Wilmington & Northern presumably felt the franchises were worth a trivial expenditure.

In 1877, just as the first Maryland & Pennsylvania was being wound up, some local businessmen led by William H. Waters of Bel Air were endeavoring to found a railroad to connect Harford County with Baltimore. S. G. Boyd, who had built the Peach Bottom, became one of the principal promoters of the new railroad. They seemed to have been interested mainly in providing an outlet for milk and other local products, but they also wanted to reach Delta, partly to tap the slate mines, partly to interchange with the Peach Bottom Railway which had reached Delta the previous year. The promoters pointed out that deposits of limestone, iron ore, chrome, manganese and asbestos lay along the proposed route. So they did, but not in economic quantities. Out of eagerness to interchange with the Peach Bottom came the decision to build the road to 3'-0" gauge. The Baltimore Towsontown Dulaney's Valley & Delta Narrow Gauge Railway Company

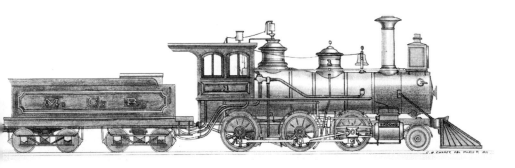

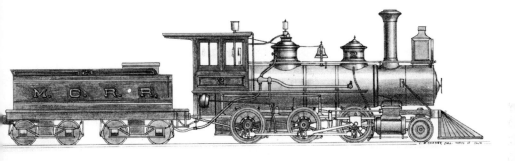

The Maryland Central's first locomotives were a pair of 2-6-0's. No. 1 came from Brooks in 1881, and No. 2 was reputed to be a Baldwin engine. *(Chaney collection, Smithsonian Institution; tickets from Charles T. Mahan, Jr., collection)*

was organized in 1876 with Waters as president, and Major Philip P. Dandridge, formerly of the B&O and the Cincinnati Southern, as chief engineer.

The new railroad, though a less ambitious project than its predecessors, did manage to be built. Since it was designed mainly for local traffic, it was laid out to serve a large number of Harford County towns. Like many railroads, it went where stock subscriptions were abundant. In particular, the railroad's promoters had a choice between a relatively direct route from Baldwin to Sharon through Pleasantville and the Twining Valley, or a tortuous line through Fallston, Vale, Bel Air and Forest Hill. Since the company could raise only $56,650 in subscriptions for the route through the lightly populated Twining Valley, but $76,000 for the line through Bel Air, the directors voted in August 1877 for the Bel Air route. Bel Air was to be their principal intermediate town, but the decision to reach it necessarily entailed building a right-of-way that would have done credit to any of the Colorado narrow gauges.

Dandridge reported early in 1878 that the railroad could be graded from Baltimore to Delta and bridge abutments could be installed for about $245,000. The directors ordered him to start locating the right-of-way immediately and turned their attention to securing an entry into Baltimore. Envisioning a narrow gauge road, they showed no interest in the Maryland & Pennsylvania's plan for building to Relay House and coming in over the Northern Central. Rather, they set out to absorb one of the lines that had been trying to establish a suburban railroad to Towsontown. The Baltimore & Swann Lake Passenger Railroad had been founded in 1868 but had accomplished little or nothing toward building a right-of-way. The company was reorganized in 1874 as the Baltimore Hampden & Towsontown Railway, and began grading for a direct 7-mile line from North Avenue in Baltimore to Towsontown. By 1878, when Waters and his friends dropped by, the grade was completed for a 3'-0" gauge line, except for about 1300 feet of trestle and five short bridges. These the BH&T hadn't the money to build, nor did the management see much prospect of raising it. The BH&T's directors were, accordingly, most receptive to the idea of a merger, and on February 5, 1878, they agreed to combine with the Baltimore Towsontown Dulaney's

Valley & Delta. On December 16 the two railroads merged to form the Baltimore & Delta Railway Company.

Meanwhile, Dandridge was in the field laying out his route. By July 1878 he upped his estimate of the costs of building to $560,000. At the end of the year most of the right-of-way was in hand, mainly acquired free from farmers. The rest was secured in 1879. In November 1878 the company issued its first offer for bids for grading. The contract was awarded to Hough, Grantz & Company of Baltimore, who for $133,000 were to grade from the Great Gunpowder River to the state line. From Swann Lake near Towsontown to the Gunpowder River, the company bought for $9500 the grade of the unbuilt Maryland & Pennsylvania.

By the end of 1879, John Hough, the contractor, had nearly finished grading from the state line through Bel Air to the Gunpowder River. In 1880, like so many other railroads, the Baltimore & Delta began to run out of funds before completion. The company decided to issue $600,000 in 6% bonds of 30-year maturity. The railroad contracted with the Baltimore banking firm of Brown & Lowndes to sell the bonds, but it proved unable to sell more than a small part of them. William Gilmor, the vice-president of the railroad, resigned his position and became agent for sale of the bonds. By offering the bonds at substantial discounts, as much as 15 per cent, he eventually disposed of $399,500 worth of them.

By the middle of 1881 Gilmor had sold about $123,000 in bonds, enough so that tracklaying could begin. The first rails were laid at Baltimore on August 23, 1881. The company hoped to have the line ready to Towsontown by November, but the first few miles out of Baltimore were all upgrade and, in some respects, the most difficult part of the entire railroad to build. The line was formally opened to Towsontown on April 17, 1882. Towsontown was even then an important suburban town, and the railroad was able to begin passenger service with eight round trips per day. The promoters had visions of eventual hourly service.

Tracklaying proceeded fairly rapidly in 1882. S. G. Boyd, as superintendent of the Baltimore & Delta, pushed construction aggressively. The line was opened on August 12 to Loch Raven, eleven miles from Baltimore. This town was the site of a large municipal reservoir. There the road erected a pavilion and picnic park, which were to be a major source of excursion traffic.

Boyd's success in making the Baltimore & Delta a going concern caused the Maryland Central to return from the limbo of forgotten projects. This railroad, it will be remembered, had laid no track but had managed to get the City of Baltimore to agree to guarantee its bonds to the extent of $600,000 as soon as it had spent $500,000 on its line. Since the Baltimore & Delta had now spent well over a half-million, the directors of the dormant Maryland Central decided to initiate talks with the B&D toward merger. It was possible, though by no means assured, that the Baltimore guaranty would be extended to the merged company. On August 28, 1882, the Baltimore & Delta lost its identity and was merged into the Maryland Central Railroad. The new hopes of financial glory were quickly dashed. The Baltimore city council took a dim view of the endorsement of the bonds and declined to extend the earlier obligation to the new company. Had the city endorsed the bonds previously issued by the Baltimore & Delta, they would have risen in price from 90 to about 130, causing a quick gain of some $140,000 to the promoters. The city was not eager to cause such a windfall. The Maryland Central thought it the better part of valor not to go to court in an effort to force the endorsement, but rather tried to talk the city council into a guaranty of bonds of $250,000 as soon as the road reached Delta. The city council had some interest in another line to Philadelphia but precious little in a local line to Delta, and the guaranty evaporated.

The little railroad's progress out of Baltimore did attract the notice of the B&O, which was currently groping for an eastern connection. The B&O had recently lost the Philadelphia Wilmington & Baltimore to the Pennsylvania Railroad, and felt sorely in need of another route to Philadelphia. Owing to the great importance of the Philadelphia & Reading in the late nineteenth century, the B&O could not endure a gap from its own rails at Baltimore to the Reading's at Philadelphia. The B&O took a quick look at the Maryland Central's right-of-way curving picturesquely about the hills and concluded that, while the line might do for carting the local dairy products into Baltimore, it could never serve as part of the B&O main line.

Maryland Central rails pushed on to Glenarm (14.5 miles) by November 1882, and reached Fallston (22 miles) in April 1883. On April 4, 1883, several members of the Baltimore city

The hefty boilers of Baltimore & Delta Nos. 3 and 4 indicate they were designed for work on heavy grades. They were built as part of the Denver & Rio Grande's 200 class, and reportedly were lettered for the D&RG before being repainted and diverted to the Baltimore & Delta. According to C. B. Chaney's drawing, the engines lost their diamond stacks and had their smokeboxes extended on the Maryland Central or the Baltimore & Lehigh. *(Both, Smithsonian Institution)*

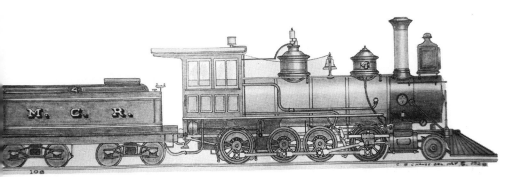

council, who were still being wooed by the Maryland Central management, were given an inspection trip to the end of track about a mile short of Fallston. The party, which numbered about a hundred, was taken on a tour of S. N. Hyde's cannery at Hyde where all were served hot corn. The railroad officials were careful to point out that Hyde planned to ship a half-million cans of corn per year over the railroad. The trip continued over the Little Gunpowder trestle, making this the first MC train to operate in Harford County. Regular passenger service to Fallston began May 7, 1883. Stages connected for Bel Air.

The tracklaying crew pushed onward, and within six weeks rails reached Bel Air, the county seat of Harford. The first train for Baltimore left Bel Air on Thursday, June 21, 1883, with four baggage cars and coaches. No ceremony had been arranged, the trip had not been advertised, and the railroad began 71 years of passenger service to Bel Air by hauling only about a dozen people on the first train. Having reached a town of some importance, the Maryland Central contracted with the Adams Express Company to handle its shipments for a standard 40 per cent of gross charges. On July 9 the Maryland Central began handling U. S. mail.

Once the Maryland Central reached Bel Air it did rather well. Its investment in right-of-way was estimated at $1 million to $1.5 million, and it had about $100,000 worth of rolling stock. The road had four locomotives, two 2-6-0's, one from Brooks and the other from Baldwin, and a pair of fat-boilered 2-8-0's which the Denver & Rio Grande had ordered from Baldwin but which had been diverted to the Baltimore & Delta on completion. Receipts ran about $250 per day, not including sale of commutation tickets. Two round trips a day were run between Baltimore and Bel Air, along with four locals to Towsontown. Since none of the locomotives was a passenger engine, the company ordered a pair of handsome 4-4-0's from Pittsburgh, Nos. 5 and 6. These were very much the pride and joy of the railroad throughout the narrow gauge era. They arrived in September 1883 and were immediately assigned to the Bel Air passenger trains.

Closing the gap between Bel Air and Delta remained before the company. This modest distance of 17 miles contained four separate summits, all with approaches of over 2 per cent, compensated. This stretch also contained some of the road's worst curvature and its biggest trestle, a vast 450-foot curved structure near Sharon. The most scenic portion of the Maryland Central also lay in this area, at Rocks in the Deer Creek gorge. The railroad attacked this terrain from north and south. In August 1883 the Maryland Central sent its locomotive No. 2 to York on a Northern Central flatcar, whence it ran over the Peach Bottom to Delta to begin construction work. Some rolling stock was sent simultaneously.

By October 5 rails had reached Forest Hill from the south, five miles beyond Bel Air and 30 miles from Baltimore. There the railroad had a celebration, complete with free lunch and band concert. The first major public meeting in support of the Baltimore and Delta had been held at Forest Hill on February 22, 1877, and about $150,000 had been raised locally. A Baltimore merchant named J. Frank Supplee, who had come to the celebration on the Maryland Central's special train, declared, not entirely without reason, that the country along the line was so lovely that he was convinced MCRR stood for "Maryland Celestial Railroad."

Meanwhile, track from the north had reached Pylesville, leaving only a seven-mile gap between the two railheads. This distance included the trestle at Sharon and the difficult grading along Deer Creek, but by December 31, 1883, the Maryland Central was able to lay its last rail on the farm of Jonathan Warner near Rocks. The line was still somewhat imperfect; in particular, it was subject to subsidence and landslides after rains. On June 30, 1883, the second car of a northbound passenger train had derailed about a mile south of Bel Air because of subsidence in the right-of-way. Delays had been frequent.

On January 21, 1884, the Maryland Central was able to begin service between Baltimore and Delta, operating two trains a day, as it was to do for many years. Running time was about three hours and ten minutes. Four days before regular service began, the railroad had a great celebration at Delta. On January 17 two of the company's locomotives hauled some 900 people to Delta on a twelve-car train. Stopping for minor festivities at towns along the way, the train took about five hours for the 44-mile trip—a bit slow even by the Maryland Central's standards. On a cold, clear afternoon, over a thousand people attended brief ceremonies out of doors. The celebrants then moved on to the basement of the Methodist Church for a banquet. At the end of the dinner, Rev. T. M. Crawford presented President Waters and General Manager Boyd with a large, fancily iced cake, lettered "MCRR-B&D". The party, doubtless pleased with the well wishes of the people of the Delta area, returned to Baltimore.

It was not long before friction was to arise between the Maryland Central and the citizenry of Delta. Sabbatarian sentiment was strong in southern Pennsylvania, though not in Maryland. The Peach Bottom never operated on Sunday, but the Maryland Central did so from the first. The Slate Ridge & Delta, which was the Maryland Central's subsidiary owning the mile of Maryland Central track in Pennsylvania, had originally stated that it would not run passenger trains on Sundays, but, doubtless for operating reasons, the company changed its mind, and operated the Sunday train into Baltimore all the way from Delta. The Delta *Herald* purported to reflect local sentiment when it wrote, "Even if corporations have no souls, this Sunday train service is an abomination that no corporation has the right to inflict on a town." The *Herald* also had a weekday grievance. Although the morning train from York and the local from Peach Bottom were scheduled to connect with the Maryland Central for Baltimore, the MC frequently left without waiting for the connections.

Somewhat more substantial objections to company policy were lurking in Baltimore. On January 21, 1884, at the first annual meeting since completion of the railroad, a group of dissident stockholders led by T. Kell Bradford attacked Waters and Boyd in protest over free issue of stock to the officers and to some of the bondholders. They sought to have the stock declared void, at least for voting at the meeting, but they were defeated. The controversy had brought out the Maryland Central's stockholders *en masse*. The meeting had begun at the North Avenue station, but the crowd was so large that it had to be transferred to the nearby Temperance Tabernacle.

Even though the Maryland Central Railroad weathered Bradford's attack, it continued to have financial difficulties. The failure to secure municipal backing of its bonds had hurt the company badly, and in spite of respectable gross receipts of $250 to $500

Nos. 5 and 6, Pittsburgh products of 1883, were the best passenger engines the Maryland Central had. The builder's photograph of No. 5 adorns the walls of the Maryland & Pennsylvania's general office to this day. (*Both, Chaney collection, Smithsonian Institution*)

Third of the Maryland Central's Pittsburgh locomotives was No. 7. Here she pauses at Towsontown while running for the Baltimore & Lehigh in the 1890's. (*W. R. Hicks collection*) Typical of the Maryland Central's passenger equipment is the Baltimore & Delta coach, below, photographed on completion at the Jackson & Sharp plant in Wilmington. (*Thomas A. Norrell collection*)

per day, the company's financial situation remained precarious. In October 1884 Spence Brown, one of the trustees under the mortgage, filed a bill in the Maryland circuit court in Towsontown for appointment of a receiver. The court responded by appointing John C. Wrenshall receiver for the Maryland Central.

The receivership of the newly-completed road was, of course, a bitter disappointment to many of its leaders. Several of the directors resigned and Boyd left the railroad permanently. Boyd returned to York, where he became editor of the York *Gazette* and a dabbler in local history. In 1890 he gave up the newspaper and took up the study of law. He was admitted to the York County bar in 1893 (at the age of 63!) and practiced until his death in 1899. In his last years his only interest in the railroad was antiquarian, but he followed its progress closely since he alone could look upon both halves of what became the Maryland & Pennsylvania as his creations.

The receivership of 1884 kept the Maryland Central from executing one of its most cherished plans, a terminal more central than the North Avenue station. Although by modern standards North Avenue is a reasonably central location in Baltimore (indeed, it is almost at the geographical center of the city), in the 1880's it was far north of the central business district. The Maryland Central proposed to build south along the Pennsylvania Railroad either into the Western Maryland's Hillen Station, or to a new terminal of its own near Hillen. In March 1884 the company managed to have introduced in the Maryland legislature a bill for municipal guarantee of $400,000 in bonds to finance the extension. Not surprisingly, the city showed as little enthusiasm for this proposal as for the earlier bond guaranties, and nothing came of the project. In the long run, the railroad need have had few regrets. The business district around Hillen Station atrophied greatly in the twentieth century, and the extension would almost certainly not have been worth the additions to the road's fixed charges.

Wrenshall paid off some $25,000 of the railroad's debts, and spent about $6000 on repairs following flood damage in August 1885. On January 19, 1886, Wrenshall requested the court to discharge him as receiver. The court accepted his report and replaced him with William Gilmor, the vice-president of the debtor company, and Samuel Spencer, an official of the Baltimore & Ohio. Gilmor and Spencer worked out a reorganization plan whereby the former common stock was wiped out, the second mortgage of $400,000 was converted into stock, and the first mortgage of $775,000 was converted dollar for dollar into new bonds. In July, after having completed his work on the refinancing, Spencer withdrew, leaving Gilmor as sole receiver.

The court ordered the Maryland Central Railroad sold at auction at Baltimore on December 10, 1888. The road was sold for $600,000 to John K. Cowen, General Counsel of the Baltimore & Ohio. A new corporation was chartered, the Maryland Central Railway Company, with Gilmor as president. The board of directors was an interesting mixture of interests that had been involved in the road's history. Gilmor represented the predecessor company. George S. Brown was connected with the investment banking firm Brown & Lowndes, which had financed the Baltimore & Delta, Cowen represented the B&O, and two men from Pittsburgh, John H. Miller and M. H. Housaman, were closely identified with the promoters of the South Penn. However diverse may have been the directors' backgrounds, they were unified by an interest in standard-gauging the railroad, combining it with the York & Peach Bottom, and pushing the tracks northeast to a connection with one of the anthracite railroads. Thus, efforts at unification, conversion and expansion were to dominate the next phase of the history of the Maryland & Pennsylvania and its predecessors.

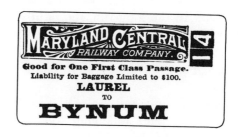

3

The Lancaster Oxford & Southern

BEFORE PROCEEDING with the history of what became the Maryland & Pennsylvania Railroad, it would be well to pause for an account of what never did become part of it: the Peach Bottom Railway's line east of the Susquehanna.

Owing to the slate deposits at Delta and the furniture factories at Red Lion, the Middle Division of the Peach Bottom proved to be a viable railroad even after the dream of a line from the Broad Top coal field to Philadelphia evaporated. No one could say the same for the Eastern Division. As it was completed from Oxford to Peach Bottom, Lancaster County, in 1878, it had nothing to support it but local farm products. The road was forced to survive on the sort of traffic that maintained the rural trolley lines in later years: local passengers picked up at every crossroad, milk from farmers, crates of eggs destined for Philadelphia via the Pennsylvania from Oxford. There was not one sizable community on the 20-mile line. The Eastern Division of the Peach Bottom had every prospect of being an epic flop, and it would be difficult to say that the road failed to live up to its potential.

The ground-breaking ceremony—the company's first misfortune—occurred on August 15, 1872, at J. M. C. Dickey's farm near Oxford. Samuel R. Dickey, who was to be the little line's most conspicuous figure, threw the first spadeful of earth. Dickey served as secretary-treasurer and as general manager from the outset. The firm of Clark & Smith had contracted for the grading. The first operation was over a three-mile stretch from Oxford to Hopewell on October 4, 1873. The main source of delay was a big trestle over Octoraro Creek.

By 1876 the railroad was nearly completed, and it enjoyed a booming business to the Philadelphia Centennial Exposition. Much of this traffic was carried free, since the railroad had traded tickets for future use in return for ties, labor, and the use of teams in grading from farmers along the right-of-way.

The Eastern Division of the Peach Bottom stayed out of bankruptcy for five years—not a bad showing, all things considered. C. W. Leavitt, a New York iron broker who had sold the company materials during construction, brought the bankruptcy action. He then bought the road at a receiver's auction on September 1, 1881. In the following month, Leavitt reorganized the line as the Peach Bottom Railroad. S. R. Dickey remained in charge of the operation.

The most conspicuous accomplishment of the Leavitt era was converting the Peach Bottom ferry to steam. Leavitt replaced the old pole ferries with a flatboat powered by a chain-driven stern wheel. Crude and ungainly as the craft was, it was the precursor of a traditional class of Susquehanna steamboats, most of which were used to dredge coal from the river near Harrisburg. Leavitt's ferry, like its successors, operated without benefit of name or registry.

In 1884 the railroad was preparing to replace the Pine Grove trestle over Octoraro Creek. All the timbers for the replacement had been laid out in the meadow along the creek when, on June 4, a flood hit the area. The timbers and the existing trestle were alike swept away. Railroad crews and local farmers recovered the new timbers, and the trestle was replaced shortly. This episode did the railroad no good, but it was a general debility of the gross receipts, rather than individual disasters, that threatened it with another bankruptcy. The line had originally run two round trips daily, but frequency rose in the 1880's to four trips. Additional trains were provided for market days. Even so, the road was eking out an existence on receipts of less than $100 per day.

A second bankruptcy was inevitable, and come it did in 1890. For the road's third try, it was reorganized as the Lancaster Oxford & Southern Railroad on September 3, 1890, under the control of Walter M. Franklin, Jacob B. Long and several other businessmen from Lancaster. They had, reasonably enough, little interest in the railroad as it was, but they conceived of it as part of an

Peach Bottom Railway

EASTERN DIVISION.

CHANGE OF HOURS.

On and after Monday, Sept. 2, 1878,

TRAINS WILL RUN AS FOLLOWS:

STATIONS	Trains Going East.		Sat. only.	STATIONS.	Trains Going West.		Mondays
	No. 1.	No. 3.	No. 5.		No. 2.	No. 4.	only.
	A. M.	P.M.	P. M.		A. M.	P. M.	No. 6.
							A. M.
Leave Dorsey's,	8.00	2.25	9.00	Leave Philadelphia,	7.00	4.30	
" Arcadia,	8.05	2.32	9.05	" Oxford,	11.20	7.30	5.20
" Westbrook,	8.10	2.38	9.10	" Hopewell,	11.28	7.40	5.27
" Eldora,	8.17	2.46	9.15	" Tweedale,	11.34	7.45	5.32
" Goshen,	8.23	2.52	9.20	" Spruce Grove,	11.46	7.55	5.42
" Fulton House,	8.30	3.00	9.25	" White Rock,	11.55	8.00	5.48
" Fairmount,	8.40	3.12	9.33	" Kingsbridge	12.05	8.08	5.54
" Kingsbridge,	8.52	3.22	9.40	" Fairmount,	12.15	8.18	6.02
" White Rock,	9.00	3.30	9.48	" Fulton House,	12.25	8.26	6.10
" Spruce Grove,	9.08	3.38	9.54	" Goshen,	12.34	8.32	6.15
" Tweedale,	9.18	3.50	10.02	" Eldora,	12.40	8.38	6.20
" Hopewell,	9.24	3.56	10.07	" Westbrook,	12.48	8.44	6.26
Arr at Oxford,	9.35	4.08	10.14	" Arcadia,	12.55	8.50	6.31
" Philadelphia,	2.37	8.55		Arr. at Dorsey's,	1.00	8.55	6.36

No. 5 and No. 6 trains will stop only when signaled.
Trains connect at Dorsey's with Columbia and Port Deposit Railroad.

August 26, 1878.

J. A. ALEXANDER, Supt.

Timetable: Smithsonian Institution.

Pass: Ward Kimball Collection.

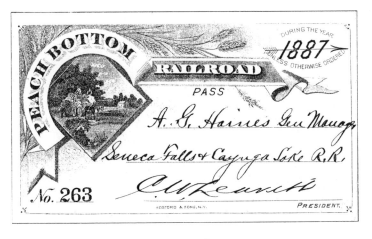

Peach Bottom enginemen Morgan Spear and James McMichael stand beside locomotive No. 2, the Porter-Bell 2-4-0 ROBERT FULTON. Superintendent John Alexander leans from the cab. *(Thomas A. Norrell collection)*

The Peach Bottom ferry was an unpretentious little stern-wheeler. A three-legged stool and a rough-hewn tiller served Captain Will Shank in place of a pilot house. *(Benjamin F. G. Kline, Jr., collection)*

outlet for Lancaster to the B&O. They hoped to acquire the Lancaster-Quarryville line of the Lancaster & Reading Narrow Gauge Railroad, which, in spite of its name, was and always had been a standard gauge operation. By building an eight-mile branch from Fairmount on the Lancaster Oxford & Southern to Quarryville, and a longer extension from Oxford to Singerly, Maryland, they would have their connection to the B&O. Indeed, one of the attractions of the bankruptcy of 1890 was giving up a charter which limited the company to branches under ten miles. The new project required conversion of the LO&S to standard gauge, either totally or at least for the easternmost 12 miles. The new owners began using standard-gauge ties for replacements on the Oxford-Fairmount sector, and throughout the 1890's they continued to plan for the conversion. The B&O actually graded four and a half miles north from Singerly in 1891, but its financial troubles of the 1890's kept it from going any further. The LO&S could never have swung the project alone.

On January 1, 1900, the Pennsylvania Railroad, which had no enthusiasm for the B&O's entry into Lancaster, took over the Lancaster-Quarryville line under a long term lease. This action effectively torpedoed Franklin's plans for the Lancaster Oxford & Southern. What was to be done with the narrow gauge now? It had been limping along on tiny gross revenues of $13,000 to $15,000 per year in the 1890's, usually losing a little but occasionally turning in a small profit. The road made $750 in 1899 — not a bad showing for a railroad with as meager prospects as this one. Franklin and his friends might have continued to operate the line as it stood, or standard-gauged it, or prepared to abandon it. What they did was the worst of all possible alternatives: they decided to build the Quarryville branch at 3'-0", and to drop plans for conversion. They had been operating with the Peach Bottom's two original locomotives, a pair of Porter 2-4-0's, plus two 4-4-0's acquired later: a Pittsburgh engine of 1885, and a Mount Savage engine bought second-hand from the West Virginia & Pittsburgh. In anticipation of a big increase in traffic, the management ordered two Baldwin 4-4-0's for 1905 delivery, Nos. 5 and 6. The road had 24 freight cars.

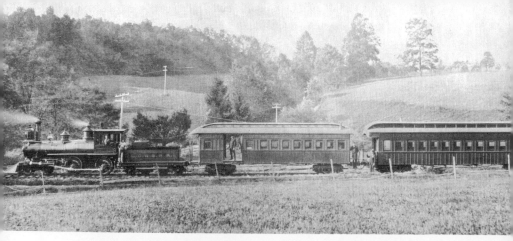

At the top, No. 3 stops at Point Lookout with a typical LO&S passenger train. *(Thomas A. Norrell collection)* At the center, No. 5 waits at Peach Bottom. The engine is one of a pair of Baldwin 4-4-0's bought at the time of the ill-conceived extension to Quarryville. *(Photograph and pass, Benjamin F. G. Kline collection)*

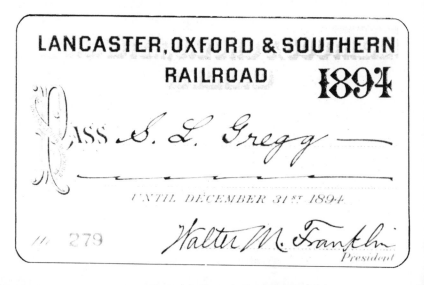

LANCASTER, OXFORD & SOUTHERN
RAILROAD   1894

Pass *S. L. Gregg*

UNTIL DECEMBER 31st 1894

Walter M. Franklin
President

279

In 1906 the Quarryville branch was opened. Once again the little road used the Pennsylvania station. Any hopes of a traffic boom must have been quickly dashed, for in 1907 the road handled 36,000 passengers at an average charge of 32 cents. Freight receipts averaged about $55 per day. The road managed to make a slight profit on this, but since the funded debt had risen to $200,000 when the branch was built, the long run prospects of success were reduced rather than increased by the new line.

The Lancaster Oxford & Southern managed to meet its fixed charges for about four years after opening the Quarryville line, but on October 1, 1910, it defaulted on the interest payments on its bonds. John A. Nauman of Lancaster was appointed receiver on March 4, 1911. The railroad was sold on March 16, 1912, to a bondholders' group, which in turn sold it in September to Fred S. Williams of Baltimore, who was affiliated with the Conowingo Power Company. The utility presumably had some intention of tying the railroad in with its power enterprises, but rapidly mounting losses caused the company to lose interest. On July 1, 1914, the railroad was closed entirely, apart from two daily round trips by a gasoline-powered speeder in fulfillment of a contract to carry the mail between Oxford and Peach Bottom.

There was still local interest in reviving the property, although it is difficult to see how anyone could have been optimistic toward it by this time. On October 1, 1914, Frank A. Patterson and some associates bought the line for $40,000 and proceeded to restore it to service. Since steam operation was proving unbearably expensive once again, the new owners sent the best of the six open-platform passenger cars to the Oxford shops to be converted to a gas-mechanical unit. The shops installed an engine in a newly-built forward compartment and arranged a chain drive to the front truck. When one of the steam locomotives cracked a frame in June, 1915, the gas car was hurriedly put into service even though its interior coachwork was not completed. The car ran on the Quarryville branch for a short period but, as usual with gas-mechanical cars of the time, breakdowns were common, and it was relegated to stand-by use.

None of the railroad was doing well, but the Quarryville branch was doing worse than the main line. World War I had so inflated the price of scrap that the owners could hardly avoid the conclusion that the branch was better off dead than alive. On April 14, 1917, No. 6 made the last trip to Quarryville, and the branch was abandoned. It brought $32,000 as scrap.

Since the traffic that supported the LO&S was of the sort most liable to highway competition, even the early motor trucks of the World War I era were enough to drive the road to the wall. Between truck competition and the high price of scrap, the LO&S did not stand a chance. Since the main line went nowhere about as completely as the Quarryville line, it did not long delay following the branch to the junk yard. Operations ceased in September 1918, and the equipment was sold at auction in October 1919. Patterson and his friends made a huge windfall gain on the scrap, reaping $250 for every $100 they had put into the road.

If the endeavors of the Ma & Pa's predecessors to convert to standard gauge are interpreted as an effort to avoid a history such as the Lancaster Oxford & Southern's, little wonder they went at it with avidity!

Conductor J. Clinton Gorsuch stands before Lancaster Oxford & Southern No. 3 with his orders in his hand. The Peach Bottom Railroad bought the 4-4-0 new from Pittsburgh in 1885. In spite of the line's chronic poverty, only one of its six engines was a secondhand purchase. (*Thomas A. Norrell collection*)

4
Unification

THE NEW Maryland Central Railway Company succeeded to what was to become the south end of the Maryland & Pennsylvania Railroad in December 1888. From the first, the new directors were eager for expansion to the north and east. Their efforts at large scale expansion, like so many earlier projects of the Ma & Pa's predecessors, foundered on the expense of bridging the Susquehanna. Although the period from 1888 through 1901 is filled with grandiose plans that came to nothing, these years are by no means an era of failure. At minimum, the men in charge did manage to convert the railroad to standard gauge and to unify the northern and southern predecessors. These were no small achievements, since as independent narrow gauges, the two predecessors would have been poor bets to last much longer than the Lancaster Oxford & Southern.

Although final unification of the Ma & Pa was a lengthy endeavor, not completed until 1901, the Maryland Central directors lost no time in trying to bring it about. As early as January 1889, Cowen and Gilmor, the heads of the Maryland Central, announced they had acquired control of the York & Peach Bottom, and they proceeded to negotiate a lease later in the year. Through service between Baltimore and York was inaugurated on May 19, 1889, and by September the two roads were being operated integrally. Two trains a day were run between Baltimore and York, scheduled for four and a half hours in each direction. There were additional locals on both ends.

Union of the north and south ends was considered the first step toward standard-gauging and operation integral with the railroad system as a whole. In particular, the Maryland Central management was eager to make the property part of a through route from the anthracite coal fields to Baltimore. Anthracite was at this time the principal fuel for domestic heating and the anthracite railroads were especially strong and powerful. By November 1889 the Maryland Central had an engineering crew out on the line making surveys for conversion.

Since the Maryland Central and the York & Peach Bottom had no physical connection with any of the anthracite railroads and had grossly inadequate terminal facilities in Baltimore, the projected expansion of the road entailed both building northward to meet the Reading and possibly some of the other anthracite carriers, and building a belt line for more complete coverage of the Baltimore area. Neither of these projects was completed, but both bulked large in the railroad's history for several years.

The proposal to build northeast to a connection with the anthracite carriers was integral with a project to build a standard gauge line from Bel Air to the Susquehanna along Deer Creek. The projected railroad, to be known as the Deer Creek & Susquehanna, was a joint enterprise of the Maryland Central and some local people, notably George M. Jewett and W. Beatty Harlan. Jewett and Harlan were interested mainly in providing service to the dairying area in Harford County between Bel Air and the Susquehanna. The DC&S was projected to run northeast 16 miles from Bel Air to the small town of Stafford at the confluence of Deer Creek and the Susquehanna River. Stafford was an even less promising terminus than Peach Bottom, but Deer Creek did provide a good descent to the river. From the first, it was proposed to build beyond Stafford, either south along the river to Havre de Grace, or northeastward to any one of a variety of points across the river. There was also talk of making connection with the Philadelphia & Baltimore Central, which terminated in Port Deposit, almost across the Susquehanna from Stafford.

The Maryland Central was mainly interested in building northeast from Stafford. Cowen and Gilmor envisioned building from Stafford up the river some four miles and there crossing to Conowingo, possibly on the existing vehicular bridge. Thence they proposed to build northeast to Coatesville where they would make their junction with the Philadelphia & Reading. From Coatesville track would run straight north, crossing the Schuylkill

River near Birdsboro, about eight miles south of Reading. The last lap would take the right-of-way through hilly country to a connection with the Lehigh Valley Railroad at Bethlehem. The track would not actually reach the anthracite region, but it would connect with at least two of the major anthracite carriers, and the Maryland Central had visions of much fruitful interchange. In retrospect the whole idea seems far beyond the company's potential, but many a less sensible project was brought to fruition in the late nineteenth century.

By January 1889 the Deer Creek & Susquehanna had let a mortgage for $300,000, and it then made a contract for grading with John H. Miller of Pittsburgh, one of the Maryland Central's directors. Miller subcontracted to L. B. McCabe & Brothers of Port Deposit, and in February grading began at Bel Air and Stafford. In the course of about three months some seven miles were graded at a cost of $67,076. The promoters hoped to have the road opened by September or October 1889, but they were unable to resume grading. Since a little less than half the right-of-way was graded, the road was far from completion. That, alas, was as far as it ever got. There were numerous reports from 1889 to 1893 that construction was about to be resumed, but all proved false. In July 1893 a Bel Air resident, Noble L. Mitchell, incorporated the Deer Creek Electric Railroad to build between Bel Air and Havre de Grace along the route of the DC&S. He proposed to have a heavy duty electric railway, capable of hauling railroad equipment in interchange, operated by hydropower from the Susquehanna. This proposal, also, came to naught. Finally in 1900, at the beginning of the interurban boom, Mitchell, Harlan, and other local figures incorporated the Bel Air & Havre de Grace Railway to build an electric line over the same route. This company managed to float a mortgage of $25,000 but never came close to building the line.

Although neither the Maryland Central nor any later company built the line, the Maryland Central wasted enough money on the project to weaken itself financially. The same might be said for the proposed Baltimore Belt Line. The Maryland Central's management could not picture the trainloads of anthracite they expected to roll down from Bethlehem terminating in the line's little yard at North Avenue. Gilmor bought a lot at Park and

Preston for an LCL house and planned a tunnel under the city to reach it. The Belt Line never got far enough along to be very clearly defined, but at the outset in 1889 it was proposed to connect with the B&O at Herring Run, and with the Philadelphia Wilmington & Baltimore at Bay View. The terminus was to be at Canton for access to tidewater. If the Maryland Central could not finance the modest Deer Creek & Susquehanna, its prospects for building this vast project in Baltimore were negligible.

The Maryland Central was nothing if not fertile with projects. The management had yet a third idea, not so monumental as the Baltimore Belt Line and the Bethlehem extension, but still enough to be beyond its capacity. The Baltimore & Delta, in pursuit of local financial support, it will be remembered, decided against a reasonably direct route between Baldwin and Sharon through the Twining Valley and built a spectacular collection of curved trestles, reverse curves and choppy grades to reach Fallston, Vale and Bel Air. This stretch was always the Ma & Pa's biggest operating headache, and as early as 1891 the Maryland Central management concluded that the whole thing would have to be straightened out. The plan was to build the direct Baldwin-Sharon line through the Twining Valley via Pleasantville. A branch would be run 2½ miles from Pleasantville south to Vale. Then the segments from Baldwin to Vale and from Bel Air to Sharon would be abandoned. Of the major towns to the line, only Fallston and Forest Hill would be cut off, and the road would be purged of uncounted degrees of curvature. The Deer Creek & Susquehanna would connect with the main line by what would be the Bel Air branch.

With the customary wisdom of hindsight, it is clear that the Maryland Central should have devoted its credit to standard-gauging what trackage it had instead of plotting schemes of the magnitude of these three.

The Maryland Central, which was at least in control of the entire line from Baltimore to York, proceeded in 1891 to merge the whole thing into a single company. On May 5, 1891, the stockholders met at Baltimore to approve the formal consolidation of the Maryland Central and the York & Peach Bottom into a single corporation, the Baltimore & Lehigh Railroad Company. Gilmor became president of the new company, and the directors

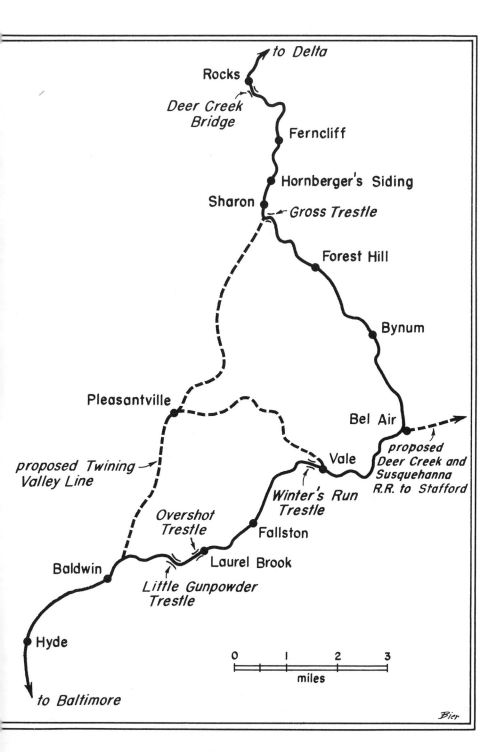

to Delta

Rocks

Deer Creek
Bridge

Ferncliff

Hornberger's Siding

Sharon

Gross Trestle

Forest Hill

Bynum

Pleasantville

Bel Air

proposed Twining
Valley Line

Vale

proposed
Deer Creek and
Susquehanna
R.R. to Stafford

Winter's Run
Trestle

Overshot
Trestle

Fallston

Baldwin

Laurel Brook

Little Gunpowder
Trestle

Hyde

to Baltimore

0   1   2   3
miles

Bier

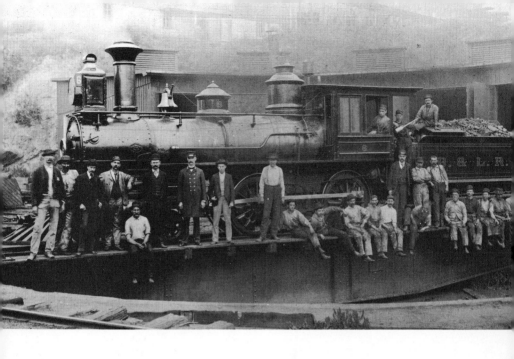

Twenty-seven Baltimore & Lehigh employees climbed aboard the Baltimore turntable to pose with No. 6. Sister engine No. 5, below, finished her days as Newport & Sherman's Valley No. 5. By the end, she had been substantially altered from her original appearance. *(Both, W. R. Hicks collection)*

The Baltimore & Lehigh bought engines 8 and 9 secondhand in the early 1890's. C. B. Chaney, who drew the plan of 9 at the top of the page, believed the engines were part of an order of 4-4-0's built by Grant for the Texas & St. Louis in 1882. Since the disadvantages of narrow gauge operation were becoming obvious, there was a heavy traffic in 3-foot gauge locomotives about the country in the 1890's as one road followed another converting to 4'-8½". *(Both, Chaney collection, Smithsonian Institution)*

represented both predecessor railroads. At the meeting yet another extension was uncorked, this time a project to build straight north from York, crossing the Susequehanna somewhere around York Haven, and then running north to Lebanon and Tremont, again to connect with the Reading and the Lehigh Valley. This route, though shorter than the proposed line to Bethlehem, would have required a crossing of Blue Mountain, probably through Swatara Gap. It would not have been easy.

Although it is unlikely that the new Baltimore & Lehigh could have accomplished much of all this at best, the company was seriously weakened by a series of accidents in the early 1890's. The new company had to contend with a series of legal actions that arose from a wreck on the Maryland Central less than a month before the railroad changed names. On April 16, 1891, unseasonably hot weather descended upon the area. The temperature stood at 84° as engine No. 3 pulled 13 cars of fertilizer northbound onto the Overshot trestle at Laurel Brook, about a mile from Fallston. Engines 14 and 2 were pushing from the rear. When the lead engine was about ten feet from the north end of the trestle, the engine crew felt the trestle begin to give way. Apparently wishing to keep the helper engines off the trestle, engineer William H. Dodson immediately whistled for brakes. His brother, James A. Dodson, the conductor, was riding in the caboose just ahead of the helper engines, talking with brakeman John Cox. Upon hearing the whistle, Cox went to the rear platform but he was too late. He saw the coupling with the engines break, just as the entire train plunged into the ravine below. Almost immediately the wreck caught fire, apparently from coals from the firebox of one of the engines. Two brakemen, John J. Martin and Benjamin Sprucebank, were killed outright. Martin, who had been riding atop one of the cars, attempted to jump free, but he was crushed by a car at the bottom of the ravine. Both Cox and William Dodson lost consciousness, but regained it in time to get out of the wreck alive. They searched for James Dodson but could not find him, and walked into Fallston to report the wreck. Later, James Dodson's remains were found in the ashes of the fire. His fireman, Charles Watts, was badly injured but he lived to be taken to the hospital. There he died the following day, leaving a widow and five children.

The Maryland Central rushed a crew to the trestle to restore it to service. There yet a fifth death occurred: Alex Johnson, a laborer, dropped dead of sunstroke on April 18 while helping to clear the wreck. The new trestle was completed on April 27. The wreck, entailing the loss of five lives, caused great local outcry. The coroner initiated an investigation and brought forth evidence damning the railroad. About a year earlier there had been complaints that the railroad's trestles were unsafe. The county engineer had given the road's trestles in Baltimore County his approval. William H. Waters, the former president of the line, testified that the trestles had been made of good white pine but that they had been intended only for about seven years of use. The original management intended to have them replaced with dirt fills but had never been able to do so. The Overshot trestle had been built in March 1883 and should, Waters thought, have been replaced about 1890. Waters had told Gilmor within the past year that many of the trestles were now unsafe.

The Harford County grand jury indicted the directors of the Maryland Central for manslaughter on the grounds of negligence. There were also civil suits against the company, especially one from William Dodson. Although injured in the wreck, he recovered. He made no effort to return to the railroad but instead became a hardware salesman, working out of Delta.

Memory of the Overshot disaster had not faded when the railroad had another trestle accident. On March 3, 1892, the Baltimore & Lehigh's afternoon passenger train from York to Baltimore left Fallston about 5:00. Just as the engine was going onto the Little Gunpowder Falls trestle, about 2½ miles south of Fallston, the baggage car derailed, dragging the engine and the smoking car off the trestle with it into the ravine. The second coach, called "the ladies' car," remained on the trestle. Engineer Henry Raab died instantly of a broken neck. Fireman George Barton made a miraculous escape by jumping onto the trestle at the instant the locomotive went over. The mail messenger, E. G. Hughes, was seriously injured. His baggage car caught fire but the crew put out the flames with milk from cans being hauled into Baltimore. Since the smoker fell about 40 feet, it was remarkable that only one passenger was seriously injured:

David Evans of Philadelphia was badly gashed in the leg by broken glass.

The railroad was again accused of negligent maintenance. Since it was known that the company intended to convert to standard gauge as soon as possible, and further, since both trestle accidents occurred on the segment that the railroad wanted to replace with the Twining Valley cut-off, local residents leaped to the conclusion that the company had intentionally neglected the line. The company, quite properly, denied these allegations. General Manager W. R. Crumpton argued that the line had kept its rolling stock in first-rate condition to facilitate sale when the road was standard-gauged. He pointed out that the B & L had been the first railroad out of Baltimore to adopt steam heat in the coaches. Had the smoker been heated with a stove, as the baggage car was, fire would almost certainly have broken out in it. The company had inspected all its trestles after the Overshot disaster and had made repairs to put them in safe condition. Crumpton pointed out that the Little Gunpowder Falls trestle had withstood the shock of the derailment perfectly.

The railroad had lost two locomotives, apparently 2 and 14, in the Overshot accident, and another, No. 16 (ex Peach Bottom No. 6) at Little Gunpowder Falls. A fire at the Falls Road roundhouse in Baltimore on October 10, 1892, cost it another locomotive, yet to be identified. It now had a motive power shortage to add to its various troubles. The 1890's were not very gay as far as economic conditions were concerned, and by 1892 the general business depression was making itself felt on the railroad. Nonetheless, the railroad had no choice but to proceed with standard-gauging.

In December 1892 the Baltimore & Lehigh signed a contract with the Baltimore Forwarding & Railroad Company which had been formed by John Henry Miller, a large B&L shareholder, to convert the railroad. For approximately $1,500,000 the Forwarding Company was to convert the line to 4'-8½", plus expand its terminal facilities. This expenditure did not include building the Baltimore Belt Line, but that project was still being considered. On January 2, 1893, the Baltimore Forwarding & Railroad Company took over the Baltimore & Lehigh. Miller became president but Crumpton remained general manager.

The glorious day when standard gauge equipment began rambling around the Baltimore & Lehigh's myriad curves was yet some years off. In 1893, a year of deep depression, the company went bankrupt as a consequence of its inability to meet fixed charges. The courts appointed separate receivers for the two segments of the line: W. H. Bosley for the Maryland trackage and Winfield J. Taylor for the Pennsylvania portion. In 1894 the two parts were sold at separate receivers' auctions, the Pennsylvania line to Warren F. Walworth of Cleveland, and the Maryland trackage to John Wilson Brown of Baltimore. Walworth, head of the Union Savings & Loan Company in Cleveland, organized the York Southern Railroad to operate the northern line. Brown, member of the prominent banking family which had participated heavily in the debtor railroad's financing, formed the new Baltimore & Lehigh Railway Company to operate the south end for the benefit of the previous bondholders.

Thus, by 1894 the work of 1891 had been undone and the two components of the Ma & Pa were again independent of one another. Walworth and Brown held talks in November and December 1894 on joint traffic arrangements. There were several evidences of friction between the two managements, however. Through passenger service was suspended and the B&L began terminating its trains at Cardiff, about half a mile south of Delta. There were local complaints about inadequate connections. More important, there was considerable difference between the two companies in financial strength. Walworth's York Southern had the stronger financial backing, the more productive tributary area, and the better physical plant. The most difficult terrain on the system was between Baldwin and Sharon, and all the major trestles were on the south end. The B&L's territory was pretty rustic, but the York Southern served some industry in the Red Lion area. Walworth had the usual ambition to reach the Reading and planned a line from York to Chickies, near Columbia, but nothing came of the proposal.

Walworth was president of the York Southern for only four years, but his administration produced one great achievement: the standard-gauging of the York-Delta line. In July 1895 it was announced that work was undertaken, and by the end of the year it had been completed. The conversion was superintended by a familiar figure, Samuel M. Manifold. Manifold, a former lieutenant in the Pennsylvania cavalry in the Civil War, had left his farm in 1872 to join the Peach Bottom Railway as an axeman. He had progressed to rodman, assistant engineer, and in 1875, chief engineer in charge of construction. He had been responsible for surveying and construction of the last 20 miles of the line into Delta. He had become superintendent of the railroad in 1877, and he became roadmaster of the combined Baltimore & Lehigh. In 1891 he left the B&L to survey a proposed extension of the Stewartstown Railroad into Delta. He next served a short time for the Pennsylvania, but when the northern segment of the future Ma & Pa again became independent in April 1893 he returned to become general manager.

The York Southern went into business as a standard gauge railroad with a trio of new Baldwin engines, two 4-4-0's numbered 1 and 3, and a 2-6-0 numbered 2. No. 3 was named for Walworth, and No. 2 for J. C. Neville, one of his associates. No. 1 was named for Manifold.

Walworth left the York Southern in 1898, transferring his interest to Daniel F. Lafean of York. This transaction precipitated a lawsuit by the Pennsylvania Railroad. The York Southern and Pennsylvania had worked closely together since 1896, when Walworth had arranged an agreement for traffic interchange at York. The Pennsylvania charged that Walworth had agreed on June 9, 1898, to sell to the Northern Central, the Pennsylvania's subsidiary, 10,000 shares of York Southern stock, and $142,000 of 5 per cent mortgage bonds for $160,000. Subsequently, Lafean had offered Walworth more favorable terms and he had accepted. The Pennsylvania remained eager to acquire control of the road, but Judge Bittenger at York refused to invalidate the sale to Lafean.

Lafean's administration, though as short-lived as Walworth's, had one major accomplishment: building a branch line into Dallastown. Although the main line had had a station called Dallastown, it was not properly in the town, and local business leaders were eager that a branch be built to serve them. Several local figures engaged Manifold to survey a line in 1893, and on October 10, 1898, the Dallastown Railroad was incorporated. Lafean was president and Manifold chief engineer, although the

The York Southern began standard gauge operation with a mogul and two Americans, all built by Baldwin in 1895. Above is the mogul, J. C. Neville, apparently photographed on arrival at York. *(W. R. Hicks collection)* American No. 1 originally bore the name S. M. Manifold, but the name was quietly dropped when Manifold began to manage the rival electric line between York and Red Lion. *(Below, Chaney collection, Smithsonian Institution)*

The Baltimore & Lehigh's No. 6 sits precariously on the ties of the Winter's Run trestle in February, 1899. The remains of No. 4 lie on the ground below. This was the last of the B&L's three major trestle derailments of the 1890's. *(W. R. Hicks collection)*

line, having been financed locally, was nominally independent of the York Southern. From the outset it was expected that the York Southern would operate the line, and it was never planned that the road would have its own rolling stock. John Dobbling of York was awarded the contract for building the line. By the standards of the Ma & Pa, the road was a modest piece of construction: 1.25 miles with a ruling grade of 2 per cent and no curve over 2°. The branch was opened May 20, 1899. Previously, on March 28, the Dallastown Railroad had been leased to the York Southern for 50 years.

The year 1898 also saw the conversion of the Peach Bottom branch of the York Southern to standard gauge. Owing to the line's light traffic, it had been allowed to remain narrow gauge for three years after the conversion of the main line. Passenger service to Peach Bottom had been discontinued in 1893, and the branch was becoming a minor part of the railroad.

By 1899 the Baltimore & Lehigh was relatively quiescent. The line was still operating as a narrow gauge. The management had bought standard sized ties and other materials for conversion, and had even let contracts on several occasions, but the road was not yet financially able to make the change. The Baltimore & Lehigh's troubles were compounded in 1899 by yet another of its characteristic accidents: a trestle derailment. In February a severe blizzard hit the east coast. Normal operations on the B&L were interrupted for several days. The superintendent sought to open the line by the expedient of having locomotives Nos. 4 and 6 push a baggage car ahead of them from Bel Air to Baltimore. This unpromising combination made it to Vale, but there the baggage car derailed upon hitting a mass of solid ice that had formed from drippings from the Vale water tank. Engineer Harry Gover on No. 4 saw what had happened, and whistled a stop signal. Engineer Blaney on No. 6 apparently misinterpreted his signal and continued forward, pushing the derailed baggage car out onto the trestle over Winter's Run. The baggage car buckled and went off into the meadow, dragging No. 4 with it. No. 6 derailed but remained on the trestle. At first it was thought that No. 4 could be salvaged, but a further fall during efforts to get her back on the track wrecked her thoroughly and she was scrapped. No. 6 was rerailed and continued in service to the end

In the early 1890's, the Baltimore & Lehigh was in the difficult situation of having a shortage of narrow gauge motive power, but not enough funds to convert to standard gauge. It bought one new locomotive in this period, No. 10, a Brooks 2-6-0 of 1893. It is shown above in an unfortunately retouched photograph in its later guise of Newport & Sherman's Valley No. 7. *(Chaney collection, Smithsonian Institution)*

No. 11 was a 2-6-0 bought secondhand in Addison, New York. This is presumed to have been Addison & North Pennsylvania No. 6, shown at upper left. The B&L's 12 and 13 are thought to be Nos. 3 and 4 of the same railroad. Compare the photograph of A&NP No. 3 at lower left *(both A&NP engines, G. M. Best collection)* with C. B. Chaney's drawing of B&L No. 12, below.

of narrow gauge operation. Gover was badly shaken up, but conductor Dan Golden was seriously injured. Although he recovered, Golden walked with a limp for the rest of his life.

About a year later the Baltimore & Lehigh finally mustered enough resources for conversion to standard gauge. At a meeting of February 3, 1900, the stockholders voted for conversion, and on April 3 work began. The railroad replaced the narrow ties with standard size and laid 70-pound rail. The work progressed rapidly, and by summer the railroad was ready for standard-gauge equipment. Narrow gauge operation ended August 22, 1900. The conversion could have taken place earlier, but the Richmond Locomotive Works was unable to deliver five standard gauge ten-wheelers until August 23. Upon their arrival the B&L discovered that they were too heavy for the track and bridges. In particular, the road found the Little Gunpowder and Winter's Run trestles and the Deer Creek steel bridge much too weak for the new engines. Even though it planned to replace these structures with new steel bridges, the railroad concluded that the five engines were too large for its purposes. Consequently, the road sold them for $56,000, just $7,000 less than they had cost. Being in immediate need of motive power, the Baltimore & Lehigh rented four engines from the B&O to provide the first standard gauge service on the line. All four were 4-4-0's of the 700 series: 718, 737, 744, and 748.

The Baltimore & Lehigh made no further effort to buy new motive power, but instead bought from the Pennsylvania Railroad three secondhand locomotives, a switcher and two road engines. The switcher, which was numbered 20, was a rare example of a saddle tank engine with a tender. It was a class A-2 0-4-0, built at the Wilmington shops of the Philadelphia Wilmington & Baltimore in 1887 for switching on some tight curves in Philadelphia. The road engines, Nos. 21 and 22, were both Altoona-built ten-wheelers of the Pennsylvania's G-2 class. The B&L paid only $9,585 for the three locomotives. With this small stable of engines, the B&L was chronically short of power, but it made no further purchases during its independent existence.

Meanwhile, events had taken place on the north end that would hasten reunification of the two railroads. In 1899 the York Southern changed hands once more, passing into control of Sperry,

The Baltimore & Lehigh had visions of beginning standard gauge operation with a set of five Richmond 4-6-0's, but they proved too heavy and had to be sold at a loss. The B&L's No. 4 is shown on the Little Rock & Hot Springs Western's turntable, bearing the Arkansas short line's No. 5. *(Charles A. Fisher collection)* The B&L was forced to begin service with rented Baltimore & Ohio equipment. Below, a five-man crew is about to set forth with B&O No. 744 and a three-car train. *(W. R. Hicks collection)*

The Baltimore & Lehigh replaced the Richmond 4-6-0's with three engines purchased secondhand from the Pennsylvania Railroad. No. 20, above, became the switcher at Baltimore. Nos. 21 and 22 were road freight engines. Below, No. 22 is decorated for a membership drive of the railroad Brotherhoods. *(Both, Chaney collection, Smithsonian Institution)*

Jones & Company of Baltimore. Lafean was replaced as president by R. L. Jones, who manifested the same interest in expansion as most of his predecessors. He sent Manifold out to survey a line from York north to meet the Reading at Bowmansdale, just west of Harrisburg. Either as an expression of contempt for the Baltimore & Lehigh's calf-path right-of-way, or as an effort to frighten the B&L into easy terms for amalgamation, Jones announced that the York Southern would consider building a line of its own from Delta to Baltimore.

Since Walworth took over the line north of Delta, the two railroads had grown successively farther apart, but once Jones assumed the presidency they moved steadily closer together. Now the two roads had yet a further incentive to combine; the interurban boom was beginning. There was danger that one or both of them would be paralleled by an electric line. In August 1899 William A. Reist, owner of the Hotel Sterling in Wilkes-Barre, proposed to build an interurban directly parallel to the York Southern from York to Peach Bottom, where he intended to build a resort hotel. He planned to build a hydro-power station at Muddy Creek Forks to generate electricity for the project. There were several plans to build interurbans between Baltimore and Bel Air.

S. M. Manifold, whose career had virtually spanned the history of the railroad, did not remain with it to see the final unification and conversion. He resigned in July 1899 to become superintendent of the Baltimore and Harrisburg divisions of the Western Maryland under his old friend, Colonel Hood. Still later, in 1904, he became general manager of the York Street Railway Company. In that capacity he was in charge of the one electric line that did compete with the Ma & Pa, the Red Lion branch of York Railways, built in 1901.

Almost simultaneously with Manifold's resignation, the York Southern had its first big wreck since standard gauge operation began. The afternoon freight bound for York encountered a landslide at Ben Roy during a violent storm on July 23. Engine No. 2 and several freight cars were derailed. Engineer Frank Jacobs was injured. Although some freight cars were junked, the locomotive was repaired and returned to service.

It takes men to run a railroad. A representative collection of Baltimore & Lehigh employees pose at York in the 1890's. From the left, at the top are Fireman Fred Kuntz, M. J. Corcoran, Jacob Gingerich, Fred Kuich, and J. H. Manifold. At the bottom are Agent E. L. Ramsey, G. W. Rupp, Dispatcher J. C. Pervis, Walter C. Myers, and John Jacobs. *(W. R. Hicks collection)*

1896   1839

York Southern Railroad

— EXCHANGE TICKET. —

Pass *R. B. Chandler Pres't.*

Postal Telegraph-Cable Co.

Countersigned   UNTIL DECEMBER 31ST 1896.

Gen'l Manager.   *W. F. Walworth*
                         President

A landslide at Ben Roy, between Red Lion and York, caused this impressive pile-up on the York Southern in July, 1899. Locomotive No. 2 was badly damaged, but repaired and returned to service. *(W. R. Hicks collection)* On the following page, ex-B&L No. 7 is working as No. 11 of the Ohio River & Western, the largest Ohio narrow gauge. *(John A. Rehor collection)*

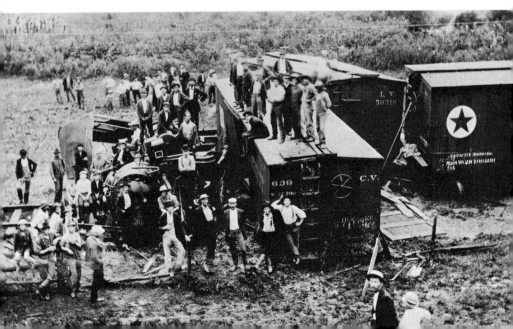

The actual unification of the two predecessors was brought about by the Baltimore investment banking firm, Alexander Brown & Company, which had previously participated in financing of the southern line. Brown offered to purchase Baltimore & Lehigh stock at $70 until March 1901. Since the conversion had been an expensive undertaking, the offer to purchase the line's stock, under the circumstances, was an attractive one. Brown bought $65,000 worth of shares and was firmly in control of the Baltimore & Lehigh.

Brown next developed a plan for a merger between the Baltimore & Lehigh and the York Southern. Brown proposed to form the Maryland & Pennsylvania Railroad with stock of $3,600,000 and bonds of the same amount. Of the common stock, $600,000 was to be distributed as a bonus to buyers of first mortgage bonds. The practice of giving away stock to purchasers of bonds is generally frowned upon as tending to create inflated capital structures, but in this instance it created a debt that the company was able to manage.

Brown's terms for merger were submitted to the York Southern's stockholders at a meeting on February 2, 1901, and approved by a vote of 11,286 shares to 400. Brown's Baltimore & Lehigh formally ratified the merger plan in a shareholders' meeting on February 12. Brown & Company's first announcement rather smacked of the old French principle, "The more things change, the more they are the same." The company announced first, that the conversion to standard gauge would be completed and second, that the road would be extended by a branch from Red Lion to Columbia, 15 miles, to connect with the Reading. The standard-gauging proceeded, but the Columbia branch went the way of all of the other proposals to meet the Reading.

Things were, however, not the same as they had been. Brown & Company had finally and indissolubly united the railroad and provided it with a capital structure that was to permit it to survive more than 60 years without bankruptcy. More important, Brown & Company provided the lovely country north of Baltimore with a standard-gauged railroad that was to serve it well for many long decades.

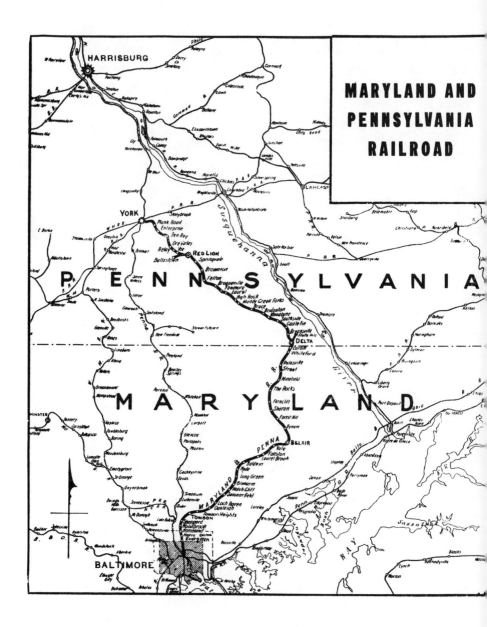

MARYLAND AND PENNSYLVANIA RAILROAD

5

The Glory Years

ONE OF THE Maryland & Pennsylvania's advantages was its timing. The line was unified at the beginning of a long period of general prosperity. From 1901, when Brown & Company put the road together, until the outbreak of the first World War in 1914, America had a lengthy era of prosperity, broken only by short-lived and minor depressions. The railroads thrived along with the rest of the economy. In the case of the Ma & Pa, the handsome earnings of these years were used to build up surpluses for debt retirement, rail renewal and for a few improvements in the physical plant.

The great improvement in the plant was, of course, completion of the conversion to standard gauge. All of the track was laid to 4′-8½″ by the time the new company was formed, but several alterations had to be made in the south end to accommodate standard equipment. Conversion of the Baltimore & Lehigh to standard gauge had entailed not only replacement of the three bridges mentioned previously, but several other line improvements as well. Trestle No. 10 at Oakleigh station was replaced with a steel viaduct and a minor relocation was made to ease curvature on the approach. The tunnel under Remington Avenue in Baltimore was so restrictive that it knocked the stove pipes off of the first standard gauge cars to run through it. The railroad decided to replace the tunnel with a cut and to build a viaduct for the street. The company also erected a train shed at North Avenue station. In 1903 the railroad spent about $100,000 on filling in the Little Gunpowder trestle and revising the approaches. The management would like to have done the same with most of the others but lacked the funds. A few revisions were made

The Ma & Pa's Baltimore station was built by the Baltimore & Lehigh. It was razed in 1937 to allow construction of the present Howard Street overpass. Thereafter, the small frame structure, below left, under the North Avenue viaduct, served as the Baltimore passenger station. *(Chaney collection, Smithsonian Institution)*

subsequently, but they were minor; in the main, the Ma & Pa had to operate with the old narrow gauge right-of-way with all its disadvantages.

It is well to pause at this point to examine in some detail the railroad that the Maryland & Pennsylvania had to operate. It was a prize. In 1924 the railroad's engineering department computed that the line had 476 curves, a neat total for a road with a 77.2 mile main line. The curves aggregated 192,261 feet, some 47 per cent of the road's mileage. Of these, exactly 100 were sharper than 14°. No less than 55 were greater than 16°. As William Moedinger, Jr., pointed out by way of contrast, the Denver & Rio Grande Western has no curve on its main line worse than 12°. The Ma & Pa's worst curve is one of 20°, about 550 feet long at milepost 50 between Southside and Woodbine, Pennsylvania. The line's engineers apparently never computed the length of the longest tangent on the railroad. They were wise in this; it certainly wasn't long enough to be worth measuring. Riding the line, particularly in the gas-electric cars in the later years, was literally tiring. One never rode for more than a few seconds without being moved to the left or to the right by a new curve. The Ma & Pa might well have called itself "The Route of the Screaming Flanges."

In addition to its excessive curvature, the Ma & Pa had to contend with fairly stiff grades. The road crossed twelve summits between Baltimore and York. There were 111 trestles and bridges.

The Ma & Pa began at a substantial stone station at North Avenue and Howard Street. The waiting room was at street level, and one descended to the trains in the shed below. The tracks were laid on the east side of the Jones' Falls valley running through the heart of the city. The Pennsylvania Railroad and the Western Maryland also occupied this valley, running on the opposite side of the creek. The Baltimore & Ohio crossed the Ma & Pa overhead north of the station. The Ma & Pa's enginehouse and its restricted yard facilities were crammed between the track and the east wall of the valley. Just north of the enginehouse, less than half a mile from the North Avenue station, the line turned right and began its ascent of a lengthy grade of about 1.7 per cent, uncompensated, up Stony Run. Considering the fre-

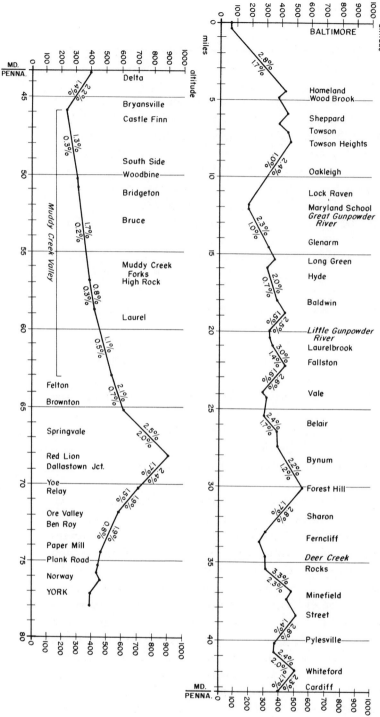

Maryland and Pennsylvania Railroad
PROFILE OF GRADES

Figures below grade line represent average grade.
Figures above grade line represent ruling grade compensated for curvature.
Basis of compensation 1° of Curve = .03% Gradient.

quency of curves on the Ma & Pa, it is pointless to talk about the uncompensated gradients. The ruling grade up from Baltimore was 2.8 per cent, compensated at the rate of .03 per cent for each degree of curvature. Being about four miles long, this was, in most respects, the most difficult grade on the railroad. The line ran through the Roland Park district of Baltimore, an elegant residential district. The Ma & Pa served no industrial areas in Baltimore and had only six industrial sidings within the city limits, of which four were coal yards serving residential areas. Thus the metropolis which the Ma & Pa served was less important as a source of traffic than the country towns between Bel Air and York.

The summit of the Ma & Pa's ascent from Baltimore was at Homeland, just short of the city limit. The line proceeded through a fairly populous suburban area to Towsontown (later Towson), one of the most important suburbs of Baltimore. Towsontown was served exclusively by the Ma & Pa and was a major source of passenger traffic. It was also a place of little importance for freight traffic since, until 1946, the railroad's only sidings ran to the state teachers' college, a lumber yard and two coal yards. There were two minor summits in this area, one at Sheppard and the other at Towson Heights, both of which were approached by short grades. From Towson Heights the line descended for about four miles to the Great Gunpowder River, and then ascended for over three miles to Long Green. This region, known as the Long Green Valley, is a high income suburban area, beautiful to the eye but, aside from a container manufacturer in Glenarm, barren of traffic prospects. In the early years this area and much of the rest of the south end of the railroad produced substantial amounts of milk for movement to Baltimore. Curvature was relatively mild in the Long Green Valley.

As the experience of the narrow gauge predecessors demonstrated, the Ma & Pa's most difficult trackage lay just beyond the Long Green Valley in the 14 miles from Baldwin to Sharon. There were three summits in this area, but the 14 miles also contained the most severe curvature on the Maryland end. The most troublesome trestles were also here. The first of the three summits was just beyond Baldwin, about 19 miles from Baltimore. There was then a short descent to the crossing of the Little Gunpowder River

A southbound freight makes its way onto the Cross trestle. The road engine will have left the trestle before the helper goes on it. (*William M. Moedinger*) The trestle could take two of the light consolidations, if separated, but the railroad avoided putting two of the 41-43 series on it.

between Baldwin and Laurel Brook. A grade of about a mile of 3.0 per cent, compensated, brought the line up to Fallston. There the railroad served a cannery which was for some years a fruitful source of freight loadings. From Fallston the railroad descended into Vale. The railroad crossed Winter's Run at Vale and began an easy ascent to Bel Air, following a tributary of Winter's Run known as Heavenly Waters.

Bel Air, with the exception of Towson, was the only sizable town on the Maryland portion of the Ma & Pa. The railroad ran through the north end of the town and served only coal yards, fuel oil depots and building supply firms. The line ran generally north to its seventh summit at Forest Hill. The descent of about 3.4 miles into the valley of Deer Creek was the ruling grade on the railroad southbound, 1.7 per cent uncompensated, and 2.8 per cent compensated—almost the same as the northbound grade out of Baltimore. About in the middle of this grade was the railroad's most spectacular structure, the Gross trestle.* The trestle crossed only a minor creek, South Stirrup Run, but it was 450 feet long with a marked curvature to the right, northbound. In two respects, the Gross trestle presented important operating problems. First, the Ma & Pa felt it desirable to prevent two locomotives being together on the trestle. Consequently, when it was necessary to double-head trains over the Maryland district, the railroad spaced the helper engine in the train, five or more cars behind the road engine. Second, the approaches to the trestle had some of the road's worst curvature. In particular, the approach from the north involved an extremely short and tight reverse curve just as the train went on the trestle.

The Sharon station was merely a flagstop at a country road, but it had some fame as the northernmost point that could be reached by a round trip from Baltimore in the late 1940's on a half-day trip on the Ma & Pa. At that time the passenger trains, morning and afternoon alike, met at Hornberger's Siding, a half mile north of Sharon. One could ride from Baltimore to Sharon, spend four minutes contemplating the trestle in the distance, and then return to Baltimore on the southbound train.

---

*This structure was frequently, but erroneously, called the Sharon trestle. According to the railroad's bridge list, the Sharon trestle was a short structure, the first trestle north of Sharon.

An early enthusiast for the Ma & Pa was the late Karl E. Schlachter, Sr. On these pages are a series of locomotive photographs he took on visits to the Baltimore yard between 1913 and 1917. The shot of No. 6 with her acetylene headlight and wooden cab (above) is notable; the engine was apparently in better condition in the 1940's than in 1917. *(Karl E. Schlachter, Jr., collection)*

All of the way from Baltimore to Ferncliff, the Ma & Pa struck out generally across the drainage pattern of the countryside. From Ferncliff to Rocks, however, the line followed Deer Creek through a narrow gorge in a mountain called Rock Ridge. This was an extremely scenic part of the line and is, in fact, now developed as a recreational area, the Rocks State Park. From Rocks the railroad followed the Gladden Branch of Rock Creek about two miles up a grade of 3.3 per cent, compensated, to Minefield. There were summits at Minefield and Street followed by a descent into Pylesville, a crossing of Broad Creek, and an ascent into Whiteford. The line was, for the Ma & Pa, fairly straight in this area. There were only about six curves in the two miles between Pylesville and Whiteford, and there were several points where a locomotive and two-car passenger train would be pulled out as straight as a pool cue.

The rest of the line may be described in the present tense, fortunately, since it is still in existence. Whiteford is the beginning of the Delta switching district. The three towns of Whiteford and Cardiff, Maryland, and Delta, Pennsylvania, are contiguous and are similar in character. Together they produce the mine products on which the Ma & Pa has always been dependent for its survival. The principal product of the area is slate granules for roofing, but at Cardiff is a quarry that produces a unique green marble. The Ma & Pa's heavy dependence on quarries made the road's earnings very responsive to the economic state of the construction business.

At the Delta station the railroad divides; the Peach Bottom branch proceeds straight ahead, but the main line turns left to begin the descent of about three miles into the Muddy Creek ravine. The Peach Bottom branch did not last long following the consolidation of the predecessor companies. Freight traffic had almost disappeared, and the branch was abandoned effective September 1, 1903. About a mile and a half of the branch was preserved to serve the Funkhouser Quarry at Slate Hill. This became a particularly valuable part of the railroad, for Funkhouser proved to be the line's most important shipper. The Funkhouser Quarry represents the east end of the Delta switching district. The entire district is covered by the same set of tariffs. The railroad also serves several small canneries in the area.

The light consolidations were the customary road freight engines of the early years. No. 23 was still capable of a turn on number 31, the York freight, in 1943. *(Charles T. Mahan, Jr.)* The Richmond Americans were the principal road passenger engines from 1901 until the coming of the gas-electrics in the 1920's. *(Chaney Collection, Smithsonian Institution)* Below is No. 5, taken in the early years of the century.

The descent to the Muddy Creek valley follows Scott Creek with a compensated grade of about 2.2 per cent. Scott Creek joins Muddy Creek between Bryansville and Castle Fin Station. The line follows Muddy Creek for about 17 miles to Felton up an easy water level grade but with incessant curvature. There are ten curves of over 18° between Delta and Laurel, all worse than any of the curves on the Maryland trackage. In general, the line follows the north bank of the creek slavishly, but at High Rock and Laurel there are cuts to avoid curvature. The two cuts at Laurel entail four crossings of the creek to gain an easy alignment, but they are, characteristically, followed by a sharp reverse curve. One of the incidental disadvantages of the Pennsylvania District is the large number of poisonous snakes in Muddy Creek. Ma & Pa track crews killed about 100 copperheads per year. Aside from a dairy in Woodbine, the towns in the Muddy Creek valley were devoid of all but the usual local traffic potential.

From Felton the railroad climbs out of the valley along Pine Run. The ascent to Red Lion from the south is the steepest uncompensated grade the railroad ever had, about 2.0 per cent. Since the curvature is easier than in the valley, the compensated grade is only about 2.5 per cent.

Red Lion was the eleventh summit on the Ma & Pa and also the highest point on the main line, 911 feet above sea level. The traffic department looked upon it as a highspot, hardly less than the operating department. The town has about 40 firms, most of which shipped on the Ma & Pa fairly regularly in the early years. Most of these were in the furniture business or in cigar manufacture. Three firms in the town made cigar boxes and there were the usual coal, lumber and feed yards. Dallastown has a similar industrial composition, with a major furniture plant and another cigar box factory. The Dallastown branch leaves the main line just beyond Red Lion. Northbound passenger trains headed up to Dallastown and backed down; southbound trains backed in and headed down.

The remaining 8 miles of the main line from Dallastown Junction into York are almost all downhill, following Mill Creek with a grade of 2.0 to 2.5 per cent, compensated. There is a minor summit coming out of the Mill Creek valley into York. As a final glory, there is a stringent reverse curve in the valley at Ben Roy.

No. 41 drags a freight southbound along Muddy Creek in 1940. William Moedinger's photograph is an excellent example of the scenery of the Pennsylvania District.

Debonaire is the word for the Ma & Pa's switchers. No. 30 rides the turntable at Eddystone on completion in 1913. *(H. L. Broadbelt collection)*

Below, a line of horses wait to load milk from Ma & Pa passenger trains at Baltimore about 1911. (*W. R. Hicks collection*) Above, No. 6, which hauled uncounted cans of the milk in her day, is turned on the York turntable. (*Robert Hanft collection*)

The line enters York from the east, runs by a large number of industrial plants, and then cuts diagonally east of the business district to a junction with the Pennsylvania Railroad just east of its station. The narrow gauge predecessors had used the Pennsylvania (Northern Central) station, but the Ma & Pa built its own depot where the line crosses Market Street. In York, the Ma & Pa at its peak served some 50 firms exclusively, most of them with private sidings. Unfortunately for the railroad, almost all of the traffic has moved only in switching movements to the Pennsylvania or to the Western Maryland, with which the Ma & Pa does not connect, but which it can reach via the Pennsylvania. Even this switching revenue has provided the Ma & Pa with an important source of income. York has usually placed third behind Delta and Red Lion as a source of freight revenue. It is notable that the Ma & Pa's "big three" traffic areas were all on the north end of the line. The south end had, at the beginning, lots of passengers, lots of milk, and lots of scenery, none of which, in the long run, were destined to do much for the railroad.

Such was the railroad that Brown & Company put together: a little bit of Colorado railroading set in the eastern hills, with slate instead of silver ore and furniture in place of sheep. That the officers kept it all going until 1958 and have kept the Pennsylvania District running up to the present, speaks extremely well for the quality of management throughout its history.

The line started its standard gauge existence with a representative of Brown & Company as president. He was J. Wilson Brown, who had headed the Baltimore & Lehigh in its later days. His had been an odd history. He was born in Baltimore in 1836, son of J. Harman Brown, a prominent member of the Brown banking family. After graduating from Princeton in 1855, J. Wilson Brown joined the B&O, but he left after four years to study theology. After a few years as a Presbyterian minister, he became deputy registrar of wills at Baltimore under his father. He then returned to railroading, becoming president of the Annapolis Washington & Baltimore Railroad, which became part of the WB&A interurban. Not one to start at the bottom, he had come to the Baltimore & Lehigh as president in 1894.

Brown's general manager was W. A. Moore, who had also come from the Baltimore & Lehigh.

The Ma & Pa's Baltimore yard and engine house were owned by the subsidiary Maryland & Pennsylvania Terminal Company. *(Left, J. H. Geissel collection)* The roundhouse served as the road's principal shop. Before it was built in 1910, motive power was shopped by the B&O at Mount Clair. *(This page, Charles T. Mahan, Jr.)*

The railroad's first order of motive power was for passenger engines from Richmond, Nos. 4-6. These locomotives were 4-4-0's, built at a time when the wheel arrangement was already obsolescent. The Ma & Pa was looking for light engines for short trains and for short wheelbases. Thus, the 4-4-0 continued to serve its needs very well. Indeed, the new engines were to serve its needs so well that No. 6 ran for over 50 years. No. 6 was to go from a beginning at which it was an engine of no particular note to an old age in the early 1950's in which it had national fame as one of the last active examples of the traditional American standard wheel arrangement. Nos. 4-6 were delivered in 1901 at a cost of $30,442, and were immediately put in service on the Baltimore-York passenger trains.

Passenger service was not much changed from the narrow gauge days. The road provided two round trips the length of the railroad, one leaving each terminal in the early morning and starting its return trip in the middle of the afternoon. These trains made the trip, including a jaunt up the Dallastown branch, in anything from 3:55 to 4:25, a slight improvement over the 4:30 of the narrow gauge predecessors. These speeds, which were well under 20 miles per hour, were hardly the sort of thing that would put the Ma & Pa in a class with the Atlantic City Railroad or the other speed specialists of the day, but the Ma & Pa had a right-of-way that wasn't exactly designed for ballast scorching. The Ma & Pa never much deviated from these schedules. By the end of passenger service in the 1950's, the run was being made in 4:10, about the same as at the outset. A friend of mine in Baltimore said that the ambition of his life was to rush into the North Avenue station with his fist full of five dollar bills, put them down on the ticket counter and shout, "Quickly, fire up No. 6, make up a special for me and take me to York as fast as you can. Money is no object. It may mean a man's life!" My suspicion is that the operating department could have broken 3:30 for him without undue risk. Unfortunately, my friend never executed his ambition to be the Death Valley Scotty of the oyster country, doubtless because he thought the whole idea would get him to the psychiatric ward long before it got him to York.

On the present freeway, one can reasonably plan on 50 minutes for the trip.

Although the two daily Baltimore-York round trips were the backbone of passenger service almost until the end, the railroad provided a variety of other trains in the early years. At the outset it ran two locals from Baltimore to Bel Air and another to Delta. It had a round trip from Delta to York, essentially providing commutation service. In 1906 the road added two more trains between Baltimore and Bel Air. One left Baltimore at 5:15 to carry commuters to the suburban towns, and another, *The Owl*, left at 11:30 p.m. to carry theater-goers. On Sunday the railroad ran two trains to Delta and one to Bel Air, but it continued to defer to sabbatarian sentiment in Pennsylvania, running nothing north of Delta.

The Ma & Pa in its early years as a standard gauge railroad had quite a variety of passenger traffic. It had the usual general traffic of traveling salesmen, relatives, shoppers, and various unclassified types. On Sundays it did a good excursion business to the hilly area between Hyde and Rocks. The milk business was little short of booming. The early morning train into Baltimore that carried most of the milk was informally called *The Milky Way*, and occasionally the entire railroad was referred to in the press in the same fashion. Between 1901 and 1914 passenger train revenues, including milk, made up about half of the road's gross.

Indeed, by 1906 President Brown felt that passenger traffic out of Baltimore was heavy enough to justify electrifying at least to Bel Air, and possibly all the way to York. Having been scorched in the narrow gauge conflagration, the road nearly went into the interurban flames. Fortunately, Brown never implemented the idea.

The Ma & Pa's first years of standard gauge operation were prosperous, indeed. Even in 1901, the first year of unified operation, the road netted over $70,000, and in the golden year of 1906 it reported net earnings of $114,913. The Ma & Pa reported a profit annually from 1901 to 1910 but paid no dividends, preferring to use its earnings for debt retirement and improvement of the line. The company built a new station at Baldwin in 1906 and made some minor line revisions at Notre Dame and Woodbrook in 1908. In the latter year the railroad organized a subsidiary, the Maryland & Pennsylvania Terminal Company, which nominally controlled its Baltimore terminal. Through the sub-

No. 6 zooms out of a reverse curve near Sheppard, Maryland, into a tangent at the Ma & Pa's usual breakneck speed of about 20 miles per hour. *(Charles T. Mahan, Jr.)*

sidiary the Ma & Pa built a direct connection to the B&O in Baltimore. There had been a connection to the Pennsylvania from the beginning. Since the terminal facilities at Baltimore were grossly inadequate, as they had been in the narrow gauge days, the road in 1910 spent over $47,000 on yards and shops at Falls Road. On the north end, all of the York-Delta main line had been converted from 56 to 70 pound rail by 1909. In 1913 the company reported it had spent $250,376 on betterments out of earnings in the past eight years.

Beginning in 1911, the Ma & Pa's reported earnings were less favorable than previously, mainly because the Interstate Commerce Commission initiated rules for depreciation accounting that were more strict than the methods the railroad had used voluntarily. In 1911, in fact, the Ma & Pa showed its first deficit, but the showing would have been poor in any case because of floods in the Muddy Creek valley in the spring. The company was back in the black for 1912, if only barely so with a net of $214. Both 1913 and 1914 produced small losses, but the company made two improvements, a 900-foot revision at Laurel to reduce a reverse curve of 19° known as "the Devil's Backbone" and reduction of an 18° curve at Rocks to 8°.

The company in the early years did not publish breakdowns of its freight traffic, but outbound movements of slate from Delta and manufactured goods from Red Lion and York rather nicely balanced inbound movements of coal. Since anthracite had not yet begun to decline as the principal home heating fuel in the eastern United States, the Ma & Pa enjoyed an inbound traffic in it to all points on the line. Given the limited potential of the Maryland District for outbound traffic, this coal movement was the major source of freight revenue south of Delta.

The secular increase in traffic up to 1914 generated a need for additional freight power. Indeed, all of the Ma & Pa's steam freight engines, save only one, dated from the period ending in 1914. Beginning in 1902, the railroad ordered eight freight engines and two switchers, all from Baldwin. First came a pair of small 2-8-0's in 1902, Nos. 23 and 24. These were little classics weighing only about 213,000 pounds. With 50-inch drivers they were hardly speed demons, but like virtually all of the Ma & Pa's steam power, they were beautifully tailored to the needs of the

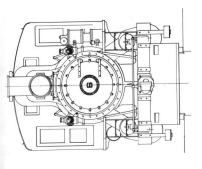

No. 6 symbolized the Ma & Pa for thousands of enthusiasts who had never seen the line. Above, the famous engine rides the Baltimore turntable in one of her most attractive portraits. (*Bert Pennypacker, H. Reid collection*) The plans, right and below, are newly executed by J. H. Geissel.

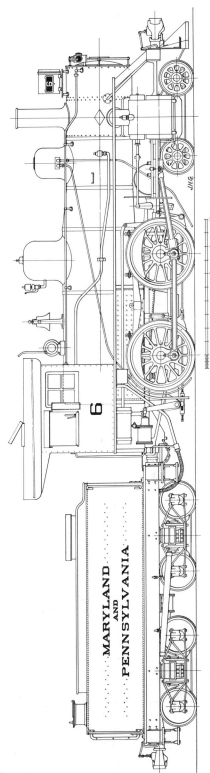

The Ma & Pa's two classes of consolidations were very different machines. Above, No. 25 pushes a cut of cars up the hill from Baltimore in the early years. (*Thomas A. Norrell collection*) Below, No. 41 waits at York before hauling number 32 to Baltimore. (*H. K. Vollrath*)

railroad. The design was duplicated in 1905 with No. 25. Next the railroad ordered a 2-6-0 which it numbered 26. This engine proved too heavy for the Ma & Pa and was sold almost immediately to the Chicago & Illinois Western.

In 1906, apparently wanting a somewhat faster freight engine capable of taking an occasional turn on the passenger trains, the Ma & Pa bought a ten-wheeler with 56-inch drivers, No. 27. The design was a success and the road duplicated it exactly in the order for No. 28 in 1910. In 1912, however, the Ma & Pa reverted to the design of the consolidations, ordering second No. 26, a duplicate of 23, 24, and 25.

By this time the Ma & Pa had no switchers. The 0-4-0st, No. 20, had been withdrawn in 1906 and not replaced. Since both York and Baltimore now had enough terminal traffic to warrant full-time switcher assignments, the road in 1913 bought a pair of similar but not identical Baldwin 0-6-0's. These were jewels of engines, in some respects the most attractive the road had. Although identical in major dimensions, 29 had Stephenson valve motion but 30 had Walshaerts motion. The difference left No. 30 about a ton heavier than 29. In addition, 29 initially had a steel cab, but 30 a wooden cab. There was no explanation of the inconsistencies. Both engines were delivered in November 1913. The Ma & Pa customarily assigned 29 to York and 30 to Baltimore, but both saw service at each terminal.

Up to 1913 all of the Ma & Pa's purchases were of engines that were hardly modern even by the standards of the day. Any of them, except perhaps 30, might easily have been built in the late nineteenth century. In 1914 the road bought two consolidations which, though necessarily short, were reasonably good examples of modern locomotives of the time. They weighed in at 316,530 pounds, a good five tons more than the heaviest of the earlier engines. With 51-inch drivers and 43,000 pounds of tractive effort, they were very well adapted to the low-speed mountain railroading of the Ma & Pa. These engines were 41 and 42, breaking the numerical sequence that had run from 20 to 30. Oddly, the numbers 41 and 42 duplicated the numbers of the daily Baltimore-York freights which the trains were intended to handle. To avoid confusion in dispatching, the trains were renumbered 31 and 32, the designation they carried to the end.

Since the three Pennsylvania Railroad engines had been retired, all the motive power was now designed exclusively for the
road's own conditions. The power had its own distinct characteristics: spoked leading wheels, relatively long smoke boxes, high
mounted headlights, number plates in the center of the smoke
box doors, and a particularly distinctive placing of the classification lamps just above the widest point on the smoke box. Since
the railroad never owned a locomotive with a trailing truck, it is
easy to dismiss Ma & Pa motive power as merely antique from the
erecting shop to the rip track. Given the nature of the terrain and
of the traffic, the motive power was very well adapted to the
needs of the railroad. With the addition in 1925 of 43, a consolidation very similar to 41 and 42, the stable of motive power of
1914 was to haul the traffic of the railroad until the post-World
War II era. The road was always given to sound locomotive maintenance, and since speed never meant much in the Ma & Pa's
calculations, the characteristics which made the engines appropriate at the outset were pretty much immutable.

The Ma & Pa in the early years acquired a substantial number
of box cars and gondolas, all of cheap wooden construction. At
the outset the Ma & Pa interchanged its cars with foreign roads,
and its box cars, particularly with loads of furniture from the Red
Lion area, circulated widely about the United States. Owing to
its heavy terminal business in coal, the Ma & Pa always had a
large number of foreign cars on the property. In one respect this
situation presented a problem to the railroad. At the time the Ma
& Pa was formed, railroads paid for the use of foreign cars on a
basis of car-miles. This was a favorable arrangement for short
lines, since foreign cars typically moved a short distance to their
destinations and then remained for several days to be unloaded.
On July 1, 1902, the railroads converted to the use of *per diem*,
the later arrangement whereby a railroad paid a flat fee for each
foreign car on its line at midnight. The change made the use of
foreign cars very much more expensive for the short lines. The
Ma & Pa was unhappy enough to build a coal tipple at North
Avenue so that foreign hoppers could be unloaded into the road's
own gondolas for delivery. The railroad saved quite a bit of *per
diem* by this arrangement in the earlier years, but toward the
end the tipple was used mainly for coaling locomotives.

The railroad adopted the car report initials "M & PA", and for many years sternly admonished readers in the *Official Railway Equipment Register* that the road must not be confused with the Missouri Pacific. This always seemed to me a bit silly. Nobody could *ever* have confused it with the Missouri Pacific.

The first No. 26 was sold almost immediately; there are no known photographs of her in Ma & Pa lettering. The locomotive went to the Chicago & Illinois Western, a subsidiary of the Illinois Central with a short mileage of switching track on the southwest side of Chicago. There, as C&IW No. 201, Robert Graham photographed the engine in the early 1930's. (*Roy W. Carlson collection*)

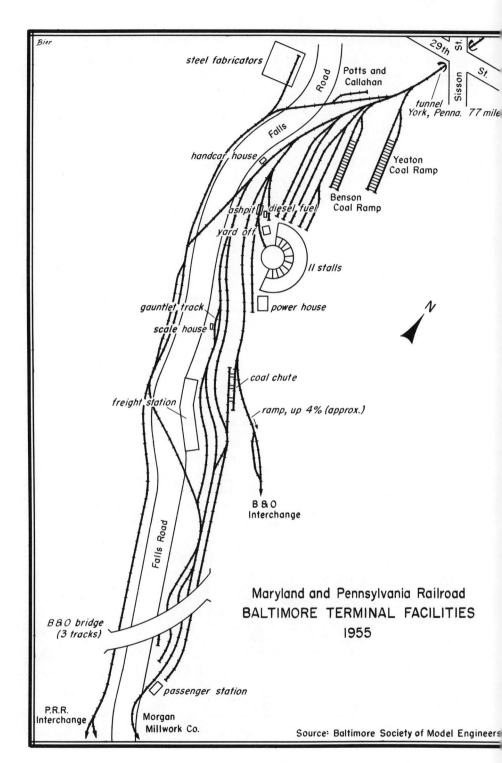

Maryland and Pennsylvania Railroad
BALTIMORE TERMINAL FACILITIES
1955

Source: Baltimore Society of Model Engineers

6

The Lean Years

ONE OF THE MOST remarkable characteristics of the Ma & Pa is the extent to which its economic fortunes have varied with the eastern railroads as a whole. Although possessed of a physical plant that looked as if Carl Fallberg or Roland Emmett had designed it, and dependent entirely on local industry, the railroad's earnings rose and fell step-by-step with other eastern railroads. This is all the more remarkable, for the Ma & Pa was mainly dependent on the slate business rather than on the steel industry, the output of which is the principal determinant of the well-being of the major eastern railroads.

Economic historians customarily date the decline of the railroads from about 1915 and, sure enough, the Ma & Pa began to decline right on schedule. In 1913 gross revenue reached a pre-World War I peak of $531,087, and the payroll reached an all-time high of 573 employees. The first blow was the completion of the state road between Baltimore and Bel Air in 1914. By 1915 there was common carrier bus service on the road and model T's were chugging along in great profusion. Milk began to move by truck as soon as the road was finished. It was not difficult for the highway vehicles of the time, however imperfect they might have been, to beat the Ma & Pa's time of 1:25 for the 26.5 mile trip. The railroad's annual report for 1915 faced up to the problem forthrightly:

"As the owner of an automobile does not ordinarily use his car simply as a matter of economy, this class of competition is one which we can hardly meet. On the other hand, automobile bus lines are a new venture, and one of doubtful economic expediency. Whether or not they will be able to compete with the railroads after proper charges for depreciation, accidents, etc., is yet an unsolved question."

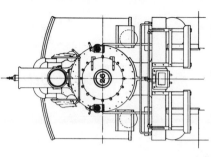

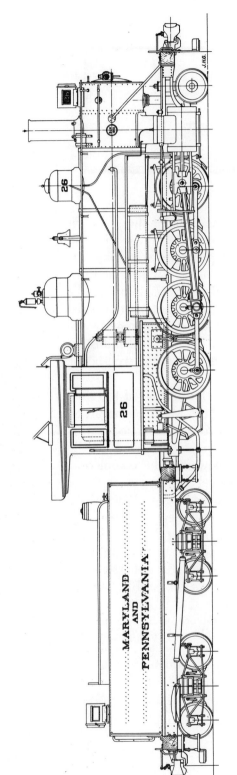

The four light consolidations are good examples of the motive power Baldwin supplied to many short lines in the pre-World War I era. The plans of 26 are by J. H. Geissel from the *Model Railroader* magazine. On the opposite page, No. 23 pulls a southbound freight past Maryland School in 1942. (*Charles T. Mahan, Jr.*)

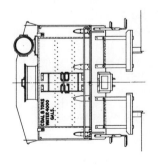

TIME SHOWN IN THIS TABLE IS STANDARD EASTERN TIME

TIME TABLE.

NORTHWARD.   **SOUTHWARD.**

SUNDAY ONLY.		DAILY, EXCEPT SUNDAY.			Distance from Baltimore.	STATIONS.	Distance from York.	DAILY, EXCEPT SUNDAY.							SUNDAY ONLY.		
57 Delta Accom.	53 Belair Accom.	51 Delta Accom.	11 Accom.	7 York Mail	3 York Mail	1 York Accom.			2 Balto. Accom.	6 Balto. Accom.	8 Balto. Mail	12 Balto. Mail	16 Delta Accom.	52 Balto. Accom.	56 Balto. Accom.	58 Accom.
P.M.	P.M.	A.M.	P.M.	P.M.	A.M.	A.M.		Leave [Arrive	A.M.	A.M.	P.M.	P.M.	P.M.	A.M.	P.M.	P.M.
4.30	12.30	8.30	5.20	2.50	7.30		77.2	Baltimore..	8.20	10.15	12.05	6.30		10.15	5.50	8.40
4.37	12.37	8.37	5.27	2.57	7.37		74.6	Evergreen...	8.09	10.05	11.57	6.20		10.07	5.39	8.33
4.44	12.44	8.44	5.34	3.04	7.44		72.9	Notre Dame..	8.04	10.02	11.54	6.17		10.05	5.35	8.35
4.46	12.46	8.46	5.36	3.06	7.46		72.1	Homeland ...	8.02	10.00	11.52	6.15		10.02	5.32	8.33
							71.0	Woodbrook ..	8.00	9.59	11.49	6.12		9.59	5.30	8.31
4.48	12.48	8.48	5.38	3.08	7.48		70.2	Sheppard ...	7.58	9.56	11.46	6.08		9.56	5.28	8.29
4.51	12.50	8.53	5.41	3.13	7.53		69.5	Towson Heights	7.55	9.51	11.44	6.01		9.51	5.25	8.26
4.55	12.57	8.55	5.49	3.15	7.55		67.6	Oakleigh ...	7.49	9.46	11.39	5.57		9.46	5.20	8.21
5.03	1.02	9.07	5.57	3.27	8.07		66.0	Loch Raven..	7.45	9.42	11.36	5.57		9.42	5.15	8.16
5.05	1.07	9.09	5.59	3.29	8.09		65.3	Maryland School	7.41	9.39	11.33	5.52		9.39	5.11	8.12
5.10	1.09	9.10	6.02	3.30	8.10		64.6	Summerfield ..	7.39	9.37	11.31	5.50		9.37	5.10	8.10
5.14	1.12	9.12	6.03	3.32	8.12		63.8	Satchan...	7.37	9.33	11.28	5.45		9.33	5.02	8.00
5.18	1.13	9.21	6.12	3.41	8.21		61.4	Long Green..	7.28	9.29	11.22	5.39		9.30	4.57	8.00
5.33	1.22	9.24	3.44	3.46	8.24		60.4	Hyde	7.24	9.27	11.20	5.36		9.23	4.54	7.57
5.36	1.33	9.36	6.30	3.54	8.40		56.0	Baldwin	7.12	9.12	11.08	5.23		9.12	4.51	7.46
5.47	1.37	9.42	6.35	3.59	8.45		54.9	Laurel Brook	7.08	9.09	11.05	5.22		9.09	4.44	7.43
5.52	1.42	9.47	6.41	4.05	8.45		58.0	Fallston ...	7.01	9.03	11.05	5.16		9.03	4.35	7.35
6.00	1.50	9.55	6.50	4.13	8.53		50.7	Belair.	6.55	8.53	10.53	5.10		8.53	4.30	7.30
6.05		10.05	6.55	4.20	8.59		48.7	Bynum		8.46	10.41	5.02		8.40	4.17	
6.20		10.10	7.15	4.28	9.00		46.9	Fork Hill...		8.24	10.31	4.47		8.40	4.08	
6.30		10.18	7.30	4.33	9.13		44.5	Sharon Hill..		8.21	10.28	4.43		8.21	4.03	
							44.5	Fern Cliff ..								
6.43		10.23	7.35	4.38	9.18		41.9	Rocks		8.15	10.21	4.38		8.15	3.58	
6.48		10.29	7.38	4.47	9.24		39.9	Minefield ...		8.04	10.14	4.31		8.04	3.50	
7.02		10.33	7.45	4.55	9.33		38.6	Street		8.00	10.10	4.28		8.00	3.46	
7.08		10.38	7.55	5.00	9.39		36.9	Pylesville ...		7.52	10.05	4.24		7.52	3.41	
							34.8	Whiteford ..		7.45	10.03	4.16		7.45	3.35	
7.11		10.47	8.01	5.03	9.42		33.9	Cardiff.	7.38	7.38	9.52	4.12		7.38	3.33	
7.15		10.50	8.05	5.08	9.50		33.4	Delta	7.35	7.35	9.45	4.10	P.M	7.35	3.30	P.M.
P.M.		A.M.	P.M.	5.12	9.55		31.8	Bryansville ..			9.31	3.31	7.20	A.M.		
				5.21	9.55		30.3	Oakland			9.30	3.52	7.00			
				5.24			27.8	Southside ...			9.30	3.52	7.00			
				5.33	10.15		26.5	Woodbine ...			9.27	3.48	6.57			
				5.41	10.20		25.6	Bridgeton ...			9.25	3.36	6.55			
				5.51	10.29		23.7	Bruce			9.12	3.29	6.50			
				5.55	10.31		21.7	Muddy Ck. Fks.			9.05	3.23	6.43			
							20.1	High Rock ..			9.03	3.16	6.39			
				6.00	10.39		17.8	Laurel			8.55	3.17	6.33			
				6.03	10.42		16.3	Fenmore			8.51	3.13	6.30			
				6.08	10.48		15.9	Brogueville ..			8.45	3.12	6.29			
				6.15	10.53		13.6	Felton			8.45	3.07	6.24			
				6.20	10.58		13.4	Bruiwtale ...			8.34	2.54	6.11			
				6.26	11.03		10.4	Red Lion ...			8.34	2.51	6.09			
				6.35	11.10		9.4	Dallastown ..			8.30	2.41				
				6.50	11.21		9.1	Yoe			8.11	2.51	6.33			
				6.51	11.29		6.9	Ore Valley ..			8.11	2.30	6.30			
				6.53	11.31		6.4	Relay			8.04	2.22	6.09			
							5.1	Ben Roy			8.02	2.20	6.05			
				6.56	11.34		4.4	Enterprise ..			8.01	2.19	5.57			
				6.58	11.36		3.9	Paper Mill ..			7.59	2.17	5.48			
				7.02	11.38		1.9	Park Road ..			7.54	2.13	5.43			
							0.8	Norway					5.31			
				7.10	11.45	7.58	77.2	York [Leave			7.50	2.10	5.35			
P.M.	P.M.	A.M.	P.M.	P.M.	A.M.	A.M.			A.M.	A.M.	A.M.	P.M.	P.M.	A.M.	P.M.	P.M.

At left is the public time table of February 15, 1924. Note that the Ma & Pa scheduled four passenger trains into Baltimore, but only three out. An early-morning freight was scheduled so that the locomotive for number 2 could arrive in Bel Air in time for the trip to Baltimore. In this period, passenger trains were handled entirely by the Americans and ten-wheelers. (*Above, Charles T. Mahan, Jr.; below, William M. Moedinger*)

When it came to freight, the Ma & Pa was no comic-opera railroad. Above, No. 41 switches box cars to the furniture factories at Red Lion. *(W. R. Hicks collection)* It was common for the passenger trains to go into the hole for freights. *(Below, William M. Moedinger)* On the opposite page, No. 42 barrels through Baldwin in 1940 with a healthy consist. *(William M. Moedinger)*

One of the Ma & Pa's most characteristic practices was renting out part of its stations for other purposes. Some had general stores or post offices, but Woodbrook doubled as a gas station. *(Charles T. Mahan, Jr.)*

The 1920's brought the last of the steam locomotives and the first of the gas-electric cars. No. 43, shown on completion at the Baldwin Locomotive Works in 1925, was handsome and powerful. *(H. L. Broadbelt collection)* Motor car 61 was neither. Its performance was so bad that it was returned to the builder almost immediately. *(Charles T. Mahan, Jr. collection)*

The problem was to get worse rather than better. In 1916 passenger revenues declined $19,000 below 1915, attributable entirely to highway competition. The road had lost $989 in 1915, but lost $2,077 in 1916. Referring again to the automobile's mordant effects on revenues, the annual report read, "We feel confident that the bottom has been reached . . ." It was not so. In 1916 regular passenger train revenues held up to the approximate level of 1915, but the road reported that the excursion business had fallen off markedly.

If revenues in these years were taking a sinister turn, the Ma & Pa made a change that, in the long run, was to be a great benefit to the road. In 1915, the company replaced J. Wilson Brown with O. H. Nance as president. Nance brought to the position a far more solid background in railroading than Brown had possessed. Nance, a Texan by birth, had begun railroading in 1898 at the age of 19 as a clerk-telegrapher on the Rock Island at Comanchee, Indian Territory. In 1902 he had moved to the Trinity & Brazos Valley at Dallas, where he rose to treasurer by 1907. He left in 1909 to become treasurer and auditor of the St. Louis Brownsville & Mexico, a position he held until he took the presidency of the Ma & Pa in 1915. Since he took office at the age of 36, it is not surprising that he was to guide the Ma & Pa's destinies for 33 years.

One of Nance's first trials was the World War I period. The Ma & Pa was taken over by the federal government on December 28, 1917, along with the rest of the American railroad system. The United States Railroad Administration was not to operate the Ma & Pa for long. The road's traffic was not of a character to boom under wartime conditions, and not even the line's most extreme enthusiasts could argue that it was exactly vital to the war effort. Consequently, on June 29, 1918, along with most other American short lines, the Ma & Pa was returned to its owners.

The road's retrenchment in these years was manifested in a slow attrition in its passenger service in the *Official Guide*. The morning local out of Baltimore to Bel Air was dropped late in 1915, and two Saturday trains to Bel Air were discontinued in 1917. There were no further reductions until February 1924, when both remaining daily locals from Baltimore to Bel Air were dropped.

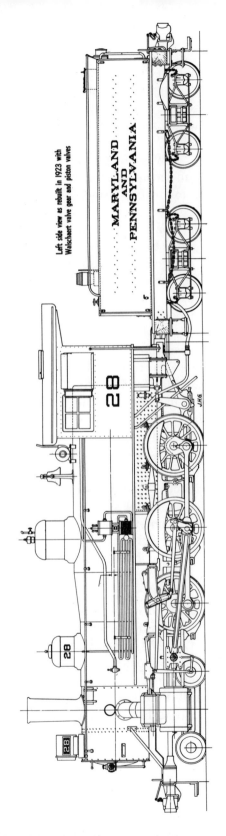

Left side view as rebuilt in 1923 with Walschaert valve gear and piston valves

MARYLAND AND PENNSYLVANIA

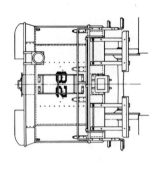

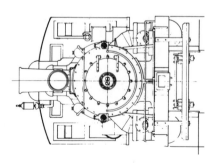

The ten-wheelers were the Ma & Pa's maids-of-all-work, handling passenger, freight and switching assignments at various periods in their long histories. (*Plans by J. H. Geissel from* Model Railroader *magazine*) For a short time in World War II they handled Sunday excursions from North Avenue for parents of boys in the Maryland Training School. No. 27 is shown at Hyde in 1942. (*Charles T. Mahan, Jr.*)

In 1920 the Ma & Pa had the only serious wreck of its standard-gauge history. Late in the afternoon of May 22 freight train number 32 was proceeding south through the Maryland District behind locomotive No. 41. The train was double-headed in the usual Ma & Pa fashion, with locomotive 26 spliced into the middle of the train. The railroad permitted crews under such circumstances to divide the train and let the lead locomotive proceed as a first section, working way freight along the line. The crew of the first section was trusted to notify opposing movements of the oncoming second section. Conductor Donnelly cut his train apart at Hyde and proposed to reunify it at Normal School Siding, 1.1 miles north of Woodbrook. He notified the dispatcher in Baltimore and ascertained that this arrangement would conflict with no northbound movements. Donnelly told head brakeman Hughes to proceed with the first section to Normal School and to wait there for the second section. Hughes apparently misunderstood instructions—he had no written orders—and believed that he should proceed as far as possible with the first section, trusting the second section to provide its own protection.

Hughes and the first section proceeded all the way to Baltimore. They arrived at 5:17 p.m., thirteen minutes in advance of the departure of the afternoon local, number 11. Hughes' engineer asked him if they should not notify the passenger crew that second 32 was still out. Hughes replied that the second section would take care of its own protection. First 32 had not carried green flags. Hughes said he had made a signal to the passenger crew but there was no indication that it was understood, if, indeed, he had made it at all.

Number 11, with engine No. 4, left on schedule at 5:30 in blithe ignorance of what was impending. Second 32 arrived at Normal School at about 5:40 after a delay because of engine trouble. Finding the first section not in the siding, the crew proceeded slowly at about 8 miles per hour, expecting to encounter the first section momentarily. Instead, they encountered number 11, traveling at the usual Ma & Pa passenger train speed of 15 to 18 miles per hour. The two trains met just south of Woodbrook at a 10° curve with a high embankment at the inside. A motorist, John Leopold of Woodbrook, who was repairing his car near the track, saw the wreck impending and endeavored to flag down the passenger train. The crew thought he was merely waving a friendly greeting and missed the last possible chance to avoid the disaster. Visibility in the curve was nil, and locomotives 4 and 26 collided head-on with terrific impact.

Charles D. Thompson, engineer of the freight, jumped free just before the impact, but John W. Blaney, his counterpart on the passenger train, was caught in the wreckage and killed instantly. Fireman Walter Mulligan of the passenger train was badly cut and bruised but was able to recover. Fireman Luther Peyton, regularly a machinist's helper at York who had been called for duty on the road only because the freight had been double-headed, had been caught by the foot between the locomotive and tender as the train was telescoped. He was in agony and it proved impossible to extricate him. It so happened that two well-known surgeons, J. M. T. Finney and William Fisher, were attending a baseball game between the Princeton freshman team and the Gilman School near the scene of the wreck. They rushed to Peyton's assistance. Finney, having nothing but a pocket knife and a saw from one of the coaches, amputated Peyton's leg at the knee to free him. Peyton was taken to a hospital, but there he died the following day.

The coroner's inquest and the ICC investigation brought forth conflicting interpretations of the causes of the wreck. The railroad insisted that orders had been issued notifying both crews of the running of the second section of the freight, but Conductor W. O. Myers of the passenger train testified that he had no reason to believe that the entire freight had not passed. Brakeman Hughes had been derelict in making no effort to inform the passenger crew of the second section, but both the coroner and the ICC held the railroad at fault for using slovenly dispatching practices and for having no adequate signals. The Ma & Pa and the Baltimore & Lehigh had permitted two-section operation of freights without classification lights and without usual methods of protection for about thirty years, but had never before encountered difficulty. The ICC recommended that the railroad adopt orthodox dispatching methods and protection for such operation, and suggested that traffic density was great enough to require manual block signals, particularly in consideration of the road's difficult terrain. The Ma & Pa did tighten its dispatch-

No. 42 pulls the time freight across the Deer Creek bridge at Rocks in one of the most attractive areas on the Ma & Pa. Above, No. 43 switches at Delta. The track directly ahead is the former Peach Bottom branch, now a spur to the Funkhouser quarry. The main line goes off to the left, just behind the tender of No. 42 in the lower photograph. *(All, William M. Moedinger)*

ing practices but continued to operate only by time table and train order.

If there was any fortunate aspect to the wreck, it was the lack of serious passenger injuries. Several passengers were badly shaken up, but the road kept its perfect record—which, indeed, it maintained to its last day of passenger service—of never having killed a passenger. In fact, this was the first head-on collision of any kind the road had suffered since it had been converted to standard gauge. Claims of all sorts and repairs to equipment cost the Ma & Pa over $47,000.

For a road which had no signals beyond a particularly simple type of order board, it was odd that the Ma & Pa had a Superintendent of Signals—and a distinguished one at that. His duties involved not oiling order boards and refilling their kerosene lamps, but rather installing and maintaining crossing protection devices. He was Charles Adler, Jr., a former Ma & Pa station agent with a considerable talent for electrical work. On February 25, 1921, he installed at the Glenarm road crossing what is widely regarded as the first American train-actuated crossing signal. It was a double stop sign which turned at right angles to the highway 20 seconds before the arrival of a train. Adler worked out the system by using the Ma & Pa's inspection car, a Hupmobile with flanged wheels, to actuate his circuits.

Adler, it might be added, went on to make a very conspicuous invention, the system of flashing lights used by aircraft in flight. He had by this time long since left the Ma & Pa, but he was publicly honored for his aircraft lighting system during World War II.

Apart from the Woodbrook collision, the Ma & Pa's principal disaster of the 1920's was a fire at the Baltimore terminal. On January 3, 1922, the fire, the origins of which were never discovered, broke out at the Baltimore freight station. The fire leveled the station to its foundation and destroyed eight freight cars and a baggage car on nearby tracks. Worse yet, the fire destroyed many of the railroad's records, creating some short-run difficulties in administration and most of the long-run gaps in the road's historical record. A new freight station was built on the foundations of the old, and in 1923 the road opened its new general offices at an expense of $36,742.

No. 100, a 1926 Rickenbacker, was the Ma & Pa's third inspection car. Previously it had used a 1916 Studebaker (No. 23, withdrawn in 1923) and a 1915 Hupmobile (No. 25, withdrawn in 1935). No. 100 did the job until 1942, and then spent another five years as a weed-burner. Since 1942, the railroad has used this 1937 Buick. It is currently equipped with two-way radio. *(Charles T. Mahan, Jr.)*

No. 61 was a typical Electro-Motive-St. Louis Car Company gas-electric of the 1920's. It is shown in the York yard in 1950, about to back down to the passenger station for a 1:10 p.m. departure. *(William S. Young)* Above, the afternoon *Baltimore Mail* loads from a Post Office truck at York in 1943. *(Charles T. Mahan, Jr.)* Below, a train pauses at Bridgeton in 1940. *(William M. Moedinger)*

Freight in the 1920's held up fairly well. The Ma & Pa built stock pens for cattle at Red Lion and Forest Hill in 1921, and in the middle of the decade built several industrial sidings, mainly in the Red Lion-Dallastown and York areas. Carload freight was proving the road's strength, but both milk and LCL were declining rapidly. In 1925 the largest milk bottler in Baltimore started using his own trucks, and the Ma & Pa was one of the railroads worst hit.

The decline in milk traffic caused further retrenchments in passenger train operation. The Baltimore-York trains were now short enough that the Ma & Pa considered converting them to gas-electric cars. The road's early experience in self-contained passenger cars had been unsatisfactory. In 1909 the Ma & Pa had leased a McKeen car for experimental operation, but it had difficulty negotiating the Devil's Backbone curve in the Muddy Creek valley just north of Laurel, and the railroad had given up on it. In 1922 the Ma & Pa tried a pair of Russell motor cars of a type that had recently been put in service on the Chicago Great Western. The first, believed to have been numbered 60, had only 60 horsepower, but the second, No. 61, had 120 horsepower and was designed to pull a trailer. Both had Wisconsin gasoline engines mounted out front in motor truck fashion. Neither car had anything approaching enough power for the Ma & Pa's conditions and both were returned to the builder almost immediately.

In 1926 the company decided to try again. The Electro-Motive Company had begun producing gas-electric cars which were proving successful for local service on railroads all over the country. Most of them were operating in the midwest, but Electro-Motive built cars to order and could be depended upon to develop a design to fit the Ma & Pa's unique requirements. The railroad ordered the car in September 1926, and in March 1927 it was delivered at a cost of $39,570. Numbered 61, it was put in service on March 23 on the round trip to York leaving Baltimore in the morning. It scraped a little of its paint on the rocks in some cuts, but it was generally acclaimed a success. It had only passenger space and it regularly towed a short baggage-RPO trailer. These trailers, which were possibly the Ma & Pa's most characteristic rolling stock, had arched roofs, truss rods and a generally homemade appearance. Their oddest feature was the use of four vertical rails spiked to each end as supports. These cars bulked large in the Ma & Pa's scheme of things, for their little RPO compartments were increasingly the source of the revenue that kept the passenger trains running.

Car 61 was successful enough that the Ma & Pa bought a second from the same builder in 1928. Although similar in passenger accommodations, the new 62 was a distillate-burner with about double the horsepower of 61. No. 62 was delivered December 30, 1928, with a price tag of $60,869. The Ma & Pa based 61 in Baltimore and 62 in York, since the morning train out of York regularly handled one or two head-end cars to Red Lion and Dallastown in addition to the York-Baltimore RPO. On its return in the afternoon, No. 62 picked up these cars for return to York. The only steam passenger trains left were the Baltimore-Delta and York-Delta commuter locals.

By the late 1920's motive power consisted of three Americans, two ten-wheelers, a pair of six-wheel switchers, and seven consolidations, including the new Baldwin 2-8-0 of 1925, No. 43. The three engines inherited from the York Southern had been retired, No. 3 in 1920, No. 1 in 1921, and No. 2 in 1927. The road did quite a bit of modernizing of the older power, applying Walshaerts valve motion, electric headlights and power reverse gears to several of the freight engines.

During the late 1920's and even into the first two years of the depression, the Ma & Pa did very well, finishing solidly in the black. For reasons that were hardly its own doing, 1930 proved to be the best year in the road's history. The Ma & Pa received a lump sum of $41,771 in retroactive mail pay for the period April 1925-July 1928. Between favorable earnings on freight and switching in 1929, and this non-recurring item, the Ma & Pa declared the first dividend in its history, $4 per share, on April 10, 1930. The road followed this with dividends of $2 on October 10, 1930, and April 10, 1931. Had the directors had any notion of what was impending, they would undoubtedly have preserved these funds. The dividend of 1931 was the last the road paid during the depression or, as it proved, during its entire history.

The close parallel between the Ma & Pa's performance and that of the eastern railroads generally has no better demonstration than the experience of the deep depression years. The company

No. 62 was the more modern, more powerful and more attractive of the Ma & Pa's two motor cars. Above, *(Charles T. Mahan, Jr.)* it sits by the fuel pump in the noon hour after coming off the Baltimore turntable. *(Below, H. K. Vollrath)* A comparison of these photographs of the postwar years reveal only a small number of changes from the original plan on the front endpaper. Drop sashes were added to the center front windows to improve ventilation.

Few photographers have ever captured the Ma & Pa's atmosphere as effectively as Charles Mahan in his shot of No. 62 at the right. Running as train number 7, No. 62 has just met No. 61 at Hornberger's Siding, and is crossing Stirrup Run Trestle en route to Delta and York.

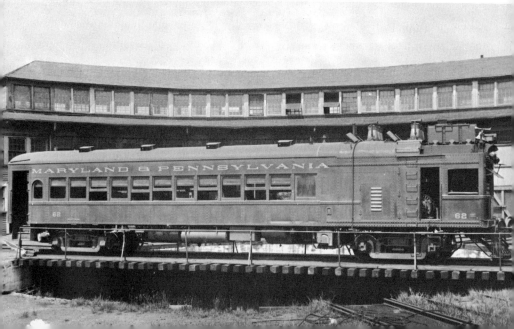

earned 2.0 times fixed charges in 1930, but only 1.11 times in 1931, about typical performances. In 1932, when the depression descended in earnest, the Ma & Pa's operating revenues fell 24.68 per cent below 1931; all class I roads' operating revenues declined by 25.4 per cent. The Ma & Pa in 1932 went into the red for the first time in the depression, losing $2,859. By 1935 the company reported the depression had cut its gross in half.

Generally speaking, the Ma & Pa's financial performance during the depression is best characterized as barely squeaking through. The road managed to cover its fixed charges by a mixture of Spartan operation, friendly relations with creditors, and a loan of $947,000 from the Reconstruction Finance Corporation. Staying out of receivership was no mean trick, for many a more promising property than the Ma & Pa was in the hands of trustees ere 1940 dawned.

In addition to the general woes of the depression, diversion of traffic to trucks increased in the 1930's. The company reported in 1933 that slate amounted to 26.06 per cent of total freight, with bituminous coal 18.56 per cent, anthracite 8.09 per cent, lumber 8.12 per cent and petroleum 11.64 per cent. All LCL had shrunk to a mere 3.54 per cent of total tonnage. If slate had always been the Ma & Pa's bread and butter, it was rapidly becoming the rest of the company's diet, too. By 1936 slate, which was not liable to highway competition, amounted to 46 per cent of all freight. Passenger trains now produced only about 11 per cent of total revenue.

The growing dependence on slate traffic gave the Ma & Pa an odd relation to weather conditions: a severe storm might raise havoc with the right-of-way, but it was almost certain to create a demand for roofing slate for house repairs. In the two big storms of the 1930's, the Ma & Pa about broke even. On August 23, 1933, the eastern United States was hit by a storm of hurricane force. It was particularly severe in the Mason-Dixon area, inflicting about three million dollars damage to York. Muddy Creek flooded, knocking out the Ma & Pa for a week. The first train made it from York to Felton on August 29, and mail service was restored the length of the railroad on the 30th. The great hurricane of 1938 struck with its maximum force to the north of the Ma & Pa, and let the road off fairly easily. In this instance the

No. 27 blasts off with both safety valve and generator at the Delta station. *(William M. Moedinger)*

Baltimore was covered with 26 inches of wet snow at the end of March, 1942. Here No. 61 pushes through it into Towson station on the morning run to York. *(Charles T. Mahan, Jr.)*

The York yard was smaller than Baltimore's, but it had its charms. Above, No. 30 steams past coach 20. The yard has two three-way switches. At the right, No. 6, filling in for No. 61, takes water at the York tank. Below, Nos. 29 and 43 line up by the tank. *(Lower right, William M. Moedinger; others, Charles T. Mahan, Jr.)*

Needless to say, railroad fans descended on the Ma & Pa in hordes. Above, a fans' special is switched at York. At lower right, No. 62 is turned for the return to Baltimore. *(Both, William M. Moedinger)* Below, enthusiasts watch No. 28 take water at the Rocks tank on an excursion of the 1930's. *(Hugh G. Boutell)* Coach 20 is preserved on the Strasburg Railroad. At upper right, No. 61 comes off the York turntable. *(W. R. Hicks)*

Railroad fans decorate 28 on an early fantrip. Below, they turn out to photograph No. 4 on the Sunday passenger train. *(Both, Hugh G. Boutell)* The heavy consolidations were anything but passenger engines, but No. 42 made a photo run for the benefit of enthusiasts. Fantrips lasted until 1947, long enough for the Diesels to handle the last one. No. 81 prepares to haul a string of Pennsylvania Railroad suburban cars out of Baltimore. *(Both, William M. Moedinger)*

Spotting the RPO for No. 62 to haul back to York was a standard noontime duty of the Baltimore switcher. Above, No. 29 does the job. *(Robert Hanft collection)* During World War II, when switching traffic at York was about the only thing that boomed on the Ma & Pa, both the switchers were assigned to the north end. The ten-wheelers were fitted with switch-engine footboards and assigned to Baltimore. Below, No. 27 pushes trailer 33 back to the passenger station. *(Harold K. Vollrath)*

demand for slate boomed, and the Ma & Pa had a more prosperous year than most of the eastern railroads.

Although the Ma & Pa made no major improvements in the depression years, the right-of-way was generally kept up, and the entire property presented a surprisingly favorable appearance. Passenger service contracted slowly. First to go was the York-Delta local in June 1930. One of the two Sunday trains from Baltimore to Delta was dropped in 1932, and the Baltimore-Bel Air Sunday local went in 1935. In December 1937 the railroad dropped the daily Baltimore-Delta train, thus ending anything in the nature of commuter service out of Baltimore. Weekday service was now limited to the two Baltimore-York round trips, known as the *York Mail* northbound and the *Baltimore Mail* southbound. The December 1937 timetable revision had one remarkable addition: the remaining Baltimore-Delta Sunday train was extended all the way to York. At this late date, the Ma & Pa began the first Sunday passenger service north of Delta in its history.

By the late 1930's, the Ma & Pa was becoming an antique that one would have to go far to match. Aside from the two gas-electrics and No. 43, there wasn't much on the property that one couldn't have seen before the *Lusitania* went down. There wasn't a single coach with an enclosed vestibule, and the freight cars were so antiquated that the Ma & Pa in April 1938 ceased sending them out in interchange. All of them had archbar trucks which were forbidden in interchange for safety reasons, and the brake equipment was no longer passable for use on foreign roads either.

The Ma & Pa's antiquity burst into full flower whenever either of the motor cars went into the shop and was replaced by one of the 4-4-0's. No. 6 was assigned to Baltimore and No. 4 to York. No. 5 was retired in 1936 and was cannibalized at Baltimore to keep the survivors going. To replace the motor car, the railroad coupled to the 4-4-0 one of the baggage-RPO's and one of the wooden coaches. Since the motor cars were out of service about 6 per cent of the time, the use of the steam train was reasonably frequent. Admittedly, one could find equal or greater antiquity elsewhere, surely on the Virginia & Truckee or the Colorado narrow gauges and possibly on some of the Georgia short lines. The

Ma & Pa, however, presented this rich show of Victorian railroading right in the heart of one of the largest cities in America, with superb scenery thrown in.

Since the 1930's kindled the first large-scale, organized railroad enthusiasm, it was natural that railroad fans would early discover the Ma & Pa. One of the first of all fan trips was held on the road in 1935, and several more were held in the late '30's. The arrival of several hundred enthusiasts on the property presented something of a problem, partly because the Ma & Pa no longer had enough coaches to handle them and partly because the curves had always been too sharp for full-length passenger cars. Fortunately, the Pennsylvania's P-54 suburban coaches were short enough for the worst curves the Ma & Pa had, and in them full trainloads of fans could be whipped off to the wilds of Harford County. The Ma & Pa operated fan trips until 1947, but unfavorable experience with theft and vandalism on the last trips caused the management to stop the practice.

World War II, like World War I, was not to do much for the Ma & Pa. Limitations on residential construction during the war prevented any boom in slate traffic, and, worse yet, outright prohibitions on short movements of oil products in tank cars cut into revenues from petroleum. Furniture loadings at Red Lion also fell to low levels. In 1943, when many railroads reached their wartime peaks of traffic, the Ma & Pa had a fall in revenue from 1942. The Ma & Pa was by this time an old hand at struggling along, and managed to survive the war years on small earnings.

The road might well have looked forward to the end of the war for release from restrictions and a chance to participate in the general postwar prosperity. Any such hopes were quickly dashed, for the postwar period proved to be the most difficult in the road's long history. After squeaking through depression and war intact and without bankruptcy, the railroad after 15 years of almost uninterrupted national prosperity found itself with its south end abandoned, and its north end barely keeping alive.

7
The Postwar Years

THE MA & PA was to find out what the postwar era had in store fast. In 1946 the road turned in a deficit of $66,298.04, the biggest in its history. Here was a loss of well over twenty times the deficit of 1932! The Pennsylvania Railroad, which had operated throughout the depression without a deficit, lost money for the first time in its entire history in 1946. Once again the Ma & Pa was going the way of the eastern railroads in general.

Much as the deficit of 1946 showed the Pennsylvania the folly of continuing to build new steam locomotives, so did it show the Ma & Pa the hopelessness of continuing to operate with the old. Neither railroad had any choice but to dieselize. The Ma & Pa enquired about for secondhand steam power in 1946, and found the Pennsylvania and B&O willing to sell some 2-8-0's and light 2-8-2's for about $40,000 apiece. Nance decided, quite correctly, that Diesels were a better buy. For the Ma & Pa, dieselization of the basic main line services could be done with a small stock of locomotives. The company in November 1946 ordered one 600-horsepower switcher, No. 70, and two 1000-horsepower switchers, Nos. 80 and 81, all from Electro-Motive. The two larger engines were intended for road service, but they were stock General Motors switchers. It was customary at that time for railroads to order longer models known as "road switchers"—what would now be called "hood units"—for road service. The longer wheelbases of road switchers made them more stable at high speeds, and the additional hood in front of the cab permitted installation of a heating boiler for passenger service. Since there was originally no expectation of using the new engines in passenger service, the railroad was not interested in heating boilers, and stability at high

The Ma & Pa was nothing if not timeless. In the 1950's, the passenger train looked much as it had early in the century. The sanserif lettering on the tender was an unfortunate economy move of the later years. *(Harry Stirton)*

speed, to put it mildly, was no problem on the Ma & Pa. Indeed, the shortness of the switchers recommended them to the Ma & Pa for operation around the curves.

Dieselization was the best thing that happened to the Ma & Pa since somebody gave it the first carload of slate. The three engines cost about $252,000, including delivery charges, but they saved about 56¢ per mile in fuel and maintenance, relative to the consolidations they replaced. The company estimated that the Diesels saved the company $45,000 per year in 1947 and 1948, permitting it to show net earnings which otherwise would have been deficits. If even a small railroad such as the Ma & Pa could show returns of this magnitude on dieselization, it was little wonder that the Diesel swept away the steam locomotive in the course of only some 15 years following the war.

Steam on the Ma & Pa lasted until 1956, however. The company, like many larger railroads, felt that it was uneconomic to dieselize all services. No. 6's stand-by duties for the gas-electrics, for example, simply did not warrant any new investment. Similarly, several of the freight engines were retained for peaks of traffic. The coming of the Diesels caused the Ma & Pa to scrap 4, 23, and 26 in 1947, but the rest of the steam locomotives went on into the 1950's.

Consequently, the arrival of the Diesels did not greatly reduce the Ma & Pa's rich antique quality. By the late 1940's, most of the rival rolling museums were either abandoned or, like the New York Ontario & Western and the Rutland, modernized in such Spartan fashion as to rob them of much of their interest. Ah, but No. 6 continued to attack the 476 curves with her traditional avidity, and steam freights were reasonably common.

Under the circumstances it was inevitable that the Ma & Pa should attract that man who savors antique railroads as he does vintage wines: Lucius Beebe. Originally, Beebe was to join an outing of prominent Baltimore society folk on May 12, 1946, but he was unable to attend. In 1947 he and his collaborator, Charles Clegg, arranged to hire No. 6, a baggage car, coach, flatcar, and caboose for an excursion in celebration of publication of their new volume on short lines, *Mixed Train Daily*.* Although the Ma & Pa

---

*MIXED TRAIN DAILY—Howell-North, 1961

In 1947, the grand life came to the Ma & Pa in the form of the Lucius Beebe excursion. At left, the train crosses the Pylesville trestle. (*Charles T. Mahan, Jr.*) Above, waiters have brought the buffet to the crew of No. 6. Below, Beebe (center, seated, with black top hat) and Charles Clegg (right, in light top hat) discuss their *Mixed Train Daily* with their guests. (*Both, Lucius Beebe collection*)

had been given relatively small notice in the book, they surely chose the proper place for their celebration. Admittedly the Ma & Pa, which had never owned a diner or an office car, was poorly equipped to provide *haute cuisine,* but ingenuity rose to the occasion, and Messrs. Beebe and Clegg provided hampers of choice foods and cascades of wine to match the flow of Deer Creek itself. The excursion went as far as Rocks, and there, amid the most spectacular scenery on the Maryland District, the party lunched on squab and champagne. Beebe and Clegg were both attired impressively in morning dress, with top hats and striped trousers. Professor Henry T. Rowell, Chairman of the Department of Classics at The Johns Hopkins University, delivered in flawless Latin a declamation in praise of the railroad. The text, unfortunately, was not recorded. The officers were duly impressed at this, for it is an honor of the sort a railroad rarely receives—no matter how much slate it hauls. On the return to Baltimore the party was serenaded by a three-piece jazz combo.

The Beebe-Clegg outing on September 14, 1947, was the ultimate recognition of the esthetic quality of the Ma & Pa. The quieter excursions of innumerable individual railroad fans on the scheduled passenger trains were a similar testimony to the road's virtual perfection from the point of view of the enthusiast. All this could not vitiate the fact that the Ma & Pa was a declining economic institution. In 1948 the company ordered two more Diesels from Electro-Motive, but earnings were so poor in 1949 that the officers cancelled the order.

At the end of the 1940's the Ma & Pa had a great blow. On June 27, 1948, O. H. Nance died of a heart attack, bringing to a close his third of a century as president. If S. G. Boyd was the principal figure of the narrow gauge days of the railroad, so was O. H. Nance the great man of its twentieth century history. He had nursed the railroad through many difficult years, and he had achieved considerable recognition in the industry. He had been chosen regional vice-president of the American Short Line Railroad Association. Since 1931 he had also been president of the Canton Railroad, an important terminal operation in Baltimore. Unfortunately, the Ma & Pa's terminal facilities in Baltimore were such that the affiliation with the Canton Railroad did the company little good.

In 1950, the U. S. Army sent one of its standard 2-8-0's, No. 2628 (Baldwin 69856, 1943), to the Ma & Pa to test the Franklin rotary cam poppet valve system. *(Below, Thomas A. Norrell collection)* Above, No. 81 helps the Army engine up the grade out of Baltimore. *(W. R. Hicks collection)*

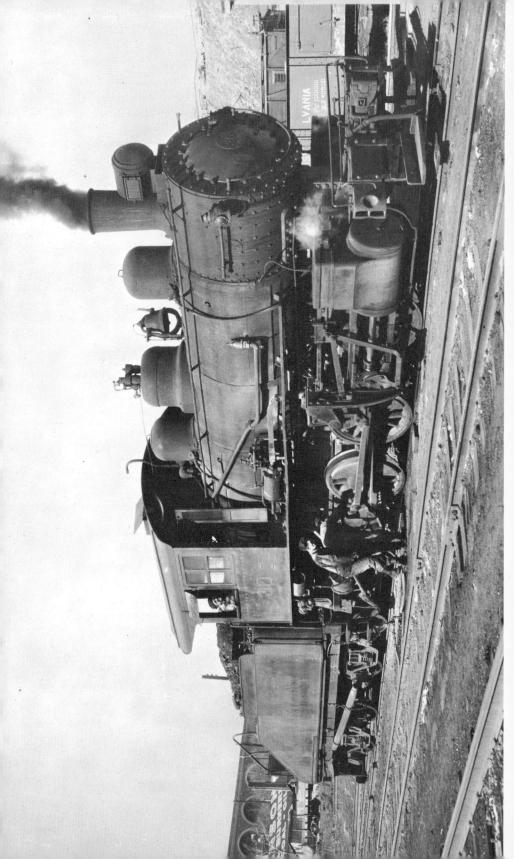

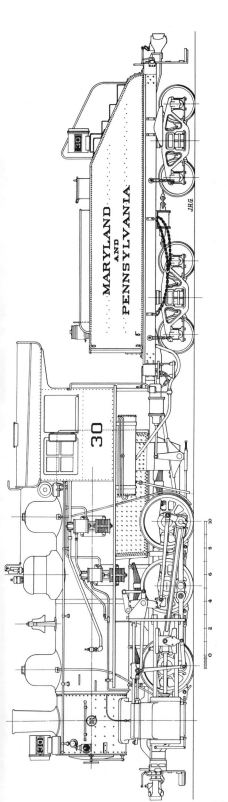

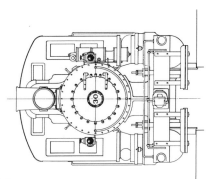

By the 1940's, the steam locomotives were spending only too much time in bad order. Above, shopmen at Baltimore inspect some minor difficulty in the grate of No. 30. (*John Pickett*) The plan of the admirable engine is by J. H. Geissel.

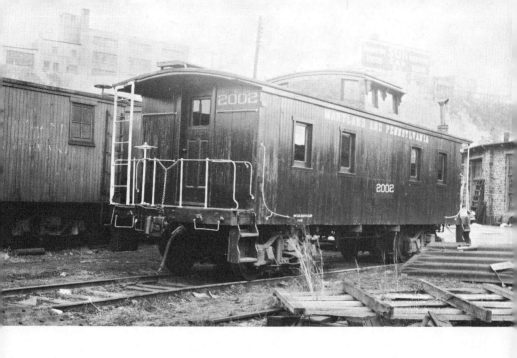

The Ma & Pa never missed a thing aesthetically. Even its cabooses looked as if they were bought to contribute to the atmosphere. Actually, the line preferred short cabooses for functional reasons; runs were so short that larger ones were not needed. (2002, *Thomas A. Norrell collection;* 2003 and 2006, *William S. Young;* 2005, *William F. Gale)*

The elder Nance was replaced as president of the Ma & Pa by his son, J. B. Nance. The younger Nance had been born in Texas in 1905, and had taken a B.S. in civil engineering at Johns Hopkins in 1926. He had then worked for the Missouri Pacific, the Kirby Lumber Company and the State of Texas before returning to the Ma & Pa in 1940. He had become vice-president and general manager in 1946, and had long been expected to assume the presidency. Although well fitted by academic training and experience for the railroad, he had less interest in keeping it operating for its own sake than many of the other officers.

The railroad suffered what was, for a company its size, a great financial setback in an accident. On January 3, 1949, Robert Hawkes, 26, a brakeman, was riding on top of a freight car when he was struck by an overhead wire and knocked to the ground. He was desperately hurt, and eventually died of his injuries in September 1950. The railroad in the interim had paid $6,500 in medical expenses. Hawkes had instituted a suit against the company for $405,000 for negligence in failing to light the wire. After his death his widow collected $67,000 from the railroad, over and above medical expenses.

The settlement of the Hawkes case was enough to put the company in the red to the extent of $29,854 in 1951. In contrast, 1950 had been an extremely good year, the best since 1930. The road had turned in a net income of $86,301 as a consequence of an upturn in freight traffic, an increase in mail rates, and a retroactive mail payment of $18,835 for the period 1947-1949. On the basis of the 1950 showing, the Ma & Pa ordered a pair of 1200-horsepower Diesel switchers from Electro-Motive. The poor showing of 1951 caused the road to cancel the order for one of the pair. The other was delivered in November 1951 at a cost of $104,700. The company sold an acre of land at Woodbrook to make the down payment. The new engine, No. 82, was expected to take over about 60 per cent of the remaining steam locomotive mileage, and turn in savings of $6000 to $8000 a year.

With the arrival of No. 82, the railroad began to retire the remaining steam power. First to go was No. 6. By this time, the little American was the last 4-4-0 in the middle Atlantic states, and one of the last few active in America. In retrospect, the scrapping of No. 6 was one of the real tragedies of the railroad. The engine needed new flues, but was otherwise in excellent condition and could easily have been preserved by an enthusiasts' group for operation. The Ma & Pa was badly enough off by this time that it could not afford the luxury of a museum piece, nor could it forego the revenue of the scrap price. The famous engine was laid up in November 1951 and scrapped in the following year. Had No. 6 survived for a few more years in the hands of a fan group, it is not difficult to envision its returning to the Ma & Pa to run Silverton-style excursions with the road's wooden coaches from York to Delta through the scenic glories of the Muddy Creek valley.

The year 1952 also saw the withdrawal of 42, the first of the heavy consolidations to go. The two remaining heavy consolidations, the two switchers and, oddly enough, the two ten-wheelers stayed on to handle whatever traffic the Diesels could not take. The railroad estimated it would take two or three more engines to dieselize completely, and the investment was not worth while. No. 82 proved money-in-the-bank, for the company estimated it saved some $20,000 in its first year of service, far more than was hoped, and permitted a profit of $27,025 in 1952.

The Ma & Pa also did well in 1953, but thereafter the downhill path was as steep as the descent from Red Lion summit. In 1954 passenger service came to an end. The Sunday passenger train had been discontinued on May 4, 1947, and on October 1, 1951, the company cut the daily passenger service from two round trips per day to one. Although the round trip from York had traditionally carried the heavier head-end traffic, the Ma & Pa chose to retain the morning run from Baltimore and the afternoon return from York. The railroad had found that only one class of passengers had remained with it in any substantial volume: domestic servants from Baltimore travelling to and from work on estates in the Long Green Valley. Many of these women lived within walking distance of the Ma & Pa's North Avenue station, and found the train an ideal way to reach work. Consequently, the railroad scheduled the morning train out of Baltimore at 7:10 so as to have them at work not long after 8:00. They could work until 4:00, catch the *Baltimore Mail* and be back in the city at 5:20 p.m. Thus, the Ma & Pa is one of the few railroads ever to provide reverse commutation service, taking passengers out of the

The agent at Glenarm holds orders for the crew of No. 6, telling them to meet No. 62, the southbound passenger train, at Rocks instead of Hornberger's Siding. The meet is at left.

Although the Diesels were not intended for passenger service, the railroad found it cheaper to run them than to use the motor cars. Consequently, on Saturdays, when there were no freight or switching duties for the Diesels at Baltimore, they frequently filled in for No. 61. Below, 81 pulls passenger train number 3 at Bel Air in 1949. *(All, including p. 140, Charles T. Mahan, Jr.)*

city in the morning and bringing them back in the afternoon. Once the railroad reduced to a single round trip, No. 62 handled the regular train, with No. 61 as its reserve, thus releasing No. 6 for scrapping.

It was, of course, the mail contract that kept the passenger trains going in the later years. Fortunately, the Ma & Pa was not directly paralleled by a highway for any long distance, and there is no road through the Muddy Creek valley. Consequently, it held its mail contract for years after RPO's had been removed from most similar operations. In the last years the railroad was hauling mail for $25,000 a year, which was enough to keep the passenger trains running on a profitable basis. In 1953 the Ma & Pa grossed $55,450 from the passenger trains, as compared with expenses of only $45,400. Passengers were down to about 12 per trip. In the middle of 1954, the Post Office Department notified the railroad of cancellation of the mail contract effective September 1, 1954. Since loss of the mail revenue would have plunged the trains immediately into the red, the Ma & Pa applied at once to discontinue them and received permission. Express revenues were falling so rapidly that the Ma & Pa's passenger service would not have lasted long in any event.

The impending end of passenger service brought the Ma & Pa a good deal of newspaper publicity, and passenger receipts were well above normal for the last week. For the last trip, on August 31, 1954, about 200 tickets were sold. The railroad used Diesel 81 to pull both motor cars, 62 and 61, and a rented Pennsylvania Railroad P-54 coach. No. 70, the York switcher, being in need of shopping in Baltimore, hauled the train back. The sounds of "Auld Lang Syne" rang through the aisles of the motor cars, each of which had turned some six million curves for the Ma & Pa. It was just over 80 years since the little RUFUS WILEY pulled the first passengers out of York.

The end of passenger service reduced receipts and costs about equally, but 1954 proved a very bad year. The company lost $42,790 and it had no alternative to drastic retrenchment. The company's decline in traffic was concentrated on the south end. Slate had passed 50 per cent of all tonnage in 1946, and by 1950 reached 58 per cent. Most of the slate moved out via the Pennsylvania interchange at York, and all of it could be routed that way.

On September 29, 1951, No. 28 pulled the last run of train number 7, the afternoon *York Mail*. The train looked appropriately wistful leaving Woodbrook. *(Charles T. Mahan, Jr.)*

Bituminous and anthracite were down to about 3 per cent of total tonnage each, and consequently, little was being terminated on the Maryland District. Milk was long since gone, and now passengers, mail and express were ending. It was no longer worth while to run a daily freight in each direction the length of the railroad, as the Ma & Pa had done for many years.

Consequently, in May 1954 the Ma & Pa began to run its freights out of York and Baltimore on a turn-around basis. The train from York ran five days a week to Delta, Slate Hill and Whiteford, and the south-end train ran from Baltimore as far north as needed. Anything moving from the Pennsylvania District south would be left by the north-end train at Pylesville or Minefield for the Maryland District train to pick up. This move permitted the railroad to economize on one train crew per day, reducing from four to three. Beginning in September 1954, a single crew alternated between switching in Baltimore and running the Maryland District freight, as traffic required. The permanent switching crew at Baltimore was discontinued forever.

Once the through freights were discontinued, the Ma & Pa's needs for motive power fell greatly. The Diesels handled nearly all the traffic, and the remaining steam locomotives were retired within three years. First to go were the ten-wheelers, 27 and 28. By the time they were scrapped in 1955, 27 was only a year short of fifty, and the oldest active locomotive in the area. In 1956 the two switchers were sold for scrap, along with consolidation No. 43. No. 41 made the last steam-powered revenue trip on November 29, 1956, and in May 1957 it followed all of the others to the rip track.

Although not one engine of the Ma & Pa was preserved, the road's motive power was yet to be immortal, if only on a small scale. Following publication of careful plans by J. H. Geissel of No. 26 in 1952 and No. 28 in 1954 in the *Model Railroader*, Japanese manufacturers brought out two HO versions of the ten-wheelers and three of the light consolidations. All of the conditions that had made the Ma & Pa's power appropriate to the Ma & Pa made it appropriate to model railroads: short curves, light tonnages, small turntables and meager budgets. By 1963 more eyes had been cast on the brass model of No. 26 than had ever seen the prototype.

By the last years, equipment about the Baltimore terminal was growing dowdy. Gondola 660 showed the effect of long years of hauling ashes. No. 4 was nearing the end of her career. The remains of No. 5 poked through the foliage beside her. *(All, Charles T. Mahan, Jr.)*

The Ma & Pa's immortality was to come in brass; below is an HO model of No. 26 by the Japanese firm of United. *(Bill Ryan, Pacific Fast Mail)*

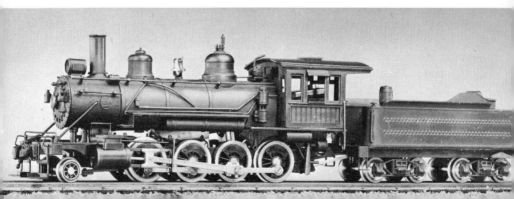

In August, 1955, No. 28 was really all dressed up with no place to go. The Ma & Pa painted her in this impressive fashion for a convention of the National Model Railroad Association. Only a month later, she was sold for scrap. At left, the engine approaches the overpass at Baldwin in 1947. The engineer is R. O. Picking, who had an excellent reputation for nursing along the old kettles in their last years. He later became the Ma & Pa's trainmaster. Below, No. 27 handles a maintenance of way extra near the Baltimore terminal. In the background is the Huntington Avenue trolley bridge. *(All, Charles T. Mahan, Jr.)*

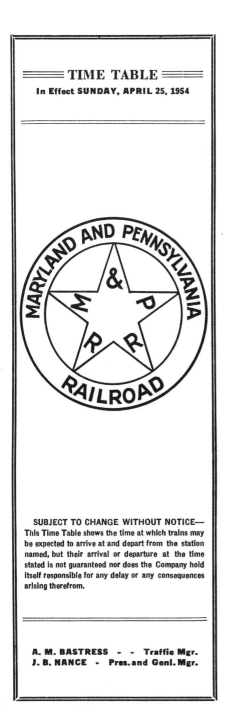

SUBJECT TO CHANGE WITHOUT NOTICE—
This Time Table shows the time at which trains may be expected to arrive at and depart from the station named, but their arrival or departure at the time stated is not guaranteed nor does the Company hold itself responsible for any delay or any consequences arising therefrom.

A. M. BASTRESS - - Traffic Mgr.
J. B. NANCE - Pres. and Genl. Mgr.

TIME TABLE
EASTERN STANDARD TIME

Effective

April 25, 1954

Read Down 1	Miles	Daily, except Sunday STATIONS	Read Up 2
Leave A. M.			Arrive P. M.
6.40	0.0	.........Baltimore.......	5.20
f 6.47	2.6	.........Evergreen.......	f 5.06
f 6.50	3.2	........Notre Dame......	f 5.04
f 6.54	4.3	.........Homeland.......	f 5.01
f 6.56	5.1	......Woodbrook	f 4.59
f 6.58	6.2	.........Sheppard.......	f 4.57
s 7.05	7.0	............Towson.......	s 4.55
f 7.08	7.7	....Towson Heights..	f 4.43
f 7.12	9.6	.........Oakleigh........	f 4.38
f 7.16	11.2	.......Loch Raven......	f 4.34
f 7.17	11.9	...Maryland School.	f 4.32
f 7.18	12.6	........Summerfield....	f 4.31
f 7.20	13.4	.........Notch Cliff.....	f 4.29
s 7.26	14.5	...........Glenarm........	s 4.27
f 7.30	15.8	........Long Green.....	f 4.23
s 7.33	16.8	...............Hyde..........	s 4.20
s 7.37	18.4	............Baldwin.......	s 4.17
f 7.43	21.2	.......Laurel Brook....	f 4.09
s 7.49	22.3	...........Fallston........	s 4.06
f 7.53	24.2	..............Vale..........	f 4.00
s 8.05	26.5	...........Bel Air.........	s 3.55
f 8.10	28.5	...........Bynum.........	f 3.45
s 8.16	30.3	.........Forest Hill.......	s 3.41
f 8.21	32.3	...........Sharon........	f 3.32
f 8.24	33.7	.........Fern Cliff.......	f 3.29
s 8.30	35.3	..............Rocks..........	s 3.25
f 8.38	37.3	.........Minefield.......	f 3.19
s 8.42	38.6	...........Street........	s 3.16
s 8.46	40.3	.........Pylesville......	s 3.11
s 8.52	42.4	........Whiteford.......	s 3.06
s 8.55	43.3	.............Cardiff.........	s 3.02
s 9.00	43.8	..............Delta........	s 3.00
f 9.05	45.9	........Bryansville......	f 2.50
f 9.08	46.9	.........Castle Fin......	f 2.47
f 9.14	49.4	.........Southside......	f 2.41
s 9.18	50.6	.........Woodbine.......	s 2.37
s 9.21	51.6	...........Bridgeton......	s 2.34
f 9.26	53.5	............Bruce.........	f 2.29
s 9.33	56.5	..Muddy Creek Forks	s 2.22
s 9.36	57.1	..........High Rock......	s 2.19
s 9.42	59.4	.............Laurel.........	s 2.13
f 9.46	60.9	.........Fenmore.......	f 2.09
s 9.50	61.3	.........Brogueville.....	s 2.08
s 9.54	63.6	.... Felton........	s 2.02
f 9.57	64.8	.........Brownton.......	f 1.57
f 10.02	66.8	.........Springvale.......	f 1.53
s 10.12	68.3	...........Red Lion.......	s 1.50
s 10.19	70.5	.........Dallastown......	s 1.38
s 10.27	70.8	..............Yoe...........	s 1.28
f 10.28	70.8	............Relay.........	f 1.26
f 10.31	72.1	...........Ore Valley......	f 1.23
f 10.32	72.8	.........Ben Roy.........	f 1.21
f 10.33	73.3	.........Enterprise.......	f 1.20
f 10.35	74.4	........Paper Mill......	f 1.16
f 10.37	75.3	.........Plank Road......	f 1.16
10.50 A. M. Arrive	77.2	..............York	1.10 P. M. Leave

f—Flag Station.   s—Stop.

Trains will stop at stations marked "f" on signal or notice to Conductor. Presentation of tickets to these stations will be considered sufficient notice.

Above is the Ma & Pa's last public timetable. Service was provided by No. 62, shown at left on one of the Ma & Pa's most notable tangents. The train is on the heavy grade northbound out of Baltimore. *(Charles T. Mahan, Jr.)*

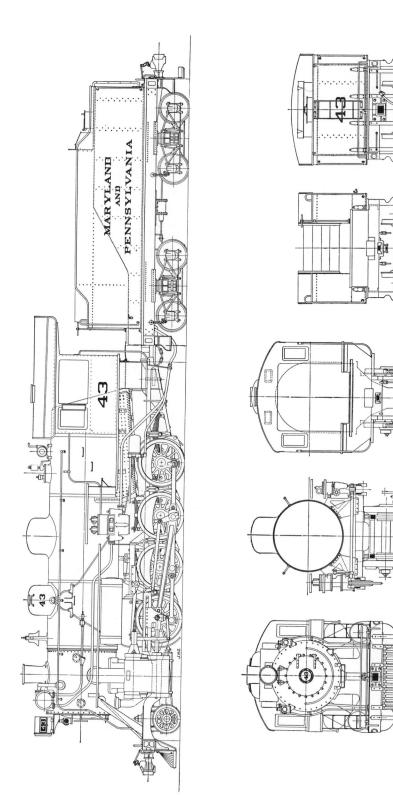

MARYLAND AND PENNSYLVANIA

43

J. H. Geissel, from the *Model Railroader* magazine.

By 1957 the Ma & Pa could handle its traffic regularly with only three Diesels, two on the north end and one on the south. In fact, the Maryland line generated so little traffic that about four trips a week out of Baltimore were enough to serve it. The one great hope for traffic on the Maryland District had come to naught. In 1946 the Bendix Corporation constructed a plant for manufacture of television sets at Towson. A siding was constructed by which for about three years the corporation received cabinets in substantial volume. Then the corporation gave up making television equipment at Towson and converted the plant into a research facility, with some general offices. The plant ceased to produce revenue for the Ma & Pa, thus gaining the same quality as practically everything else on the line south of Whiteford.

The Maryland District was dying. It had a couple of shots of adrenalin in the form of steel pipe moving in 1955 to construction sites for a transcontinental pipeline that passed through the area, and again in 1956 from movements of Indiana limestone for the new Catholic cathedral in Baltimore. That was all, however. The Ma & Pa lost $83,671 in 1955 and $122,594 in 1956. After dropping another $40,943 in the first five months of 1957, it gave up on the Maryland line, and on July 8, 1957, applied to the ICC for abandonment south of Whiteford. There was only small opposition, since all the remaining traffic could move by truck without much difficulty. The ICC granted the plea in the following year, and on June 11, 1958, the line was officially abandoned. No. 82 dragged seven cars, mostly empties, into Baltimore on the last day of revenue service. On August 5, No. 82 brought wrecking equipment and other non-revenue cars up to Delta. The line was dismantled. The 6920 feet of wooden trestle and 1735 feet of steel bridges came down, and the line was free of its worst maintenance problems.

Not the least of the Ma & Pa's troubles in its efforts to retrench was the problem of what to do with the employees. The ICC, as it frequently does with partial abandonment of weak railroads, freed the Ma & Pa from the necessity of giving extensive dismissal pay to its employees. The Ma & Pa is anything but a heartless corporation, and the average length of service of its employees is impressive. In 1949 the road awarded gold lapel buttons

At the end, the Maryland District starved for traffic. No. 81 is about to leave for Delta with one of the Ma & Pa's own vintage box cars for LCL and a B&O car in interchange. *(Thomas A. Norrell collection)* The Ma & Pa's most serious accident of recent years was a derailment of No. 82 at Oakleigh in 1953. The engine, best of the Ma & Pa's Diesels, had to be returned to La Grange for repairs. The Ma & Pa has its own big hook, but borrowed a larger one from the B&O. *(Charles T. Mahan, Jr.)*

No. 82 set out on June 11, 1958, with a Ma & Pa box car and a caboose on the last revenue trip on the Maryland District. Below, she returned to Baltimore late in the evening with six more cars, mainly empties picked up at sidings along the way. It was an historic moment when the last Ma & Pa train came into Baltimore, but few were there to see it. *(Charles T. Mahan, Jr.)*

The scrappers took over the Maryland District in the summer of 1958. Here track is removed at Towson Heights   *(Charles T. Mahan, Jr.)*

What was left was a freight two or three times weekly between York and the Delta switching area. Here No. 82 switches at the Delta station. *(Three pictures, William F. Gale)* No. 82 usually handled the road freight and No. 81 did most of the York switching.

to employees of 25 years' service. It gave out 82 buttons, four with diamond insets to mark 50 years of service. N. T. Logan, the agent at Felton, had been with the railroad since 1898; the station at Felton was closed on his retirement in 1953. The railroad laid men off on a basis of seniority, keeping its employees of longest standing to run the north end.

The snake-like quality of the Ma & Pa's right of way made the abandoned line good for not much but melancholy walks by enthusiasts. The Baltimore municipal government considered using the right-of-way out of the city for a freeway, but, since at points it was only 30 feet wide, the city traffic officials thought it of no value. A proposal that it be used as a single-lane express-way for buses also came to nothing. The city did buy the Ma & Pa's terminal facilities and part of the right-of-way in 1960 for $275,000, planning to use the roundhouse as a warehouse for the city highway department.

Out on the line several stations were preserved. The Ma & Pa had been bolstering its revenues for years by letting out parts of stations for use as stores, gas stations, and post offices. The Hyde station went its way as the local post office and general store. The stations at Long Green and Lake Avenue were cleverly de-veloped into private houses, but the Bel Air station was razed. With the abandonment of the south end, the Ma & Pa had a sur-plus of motive power; the remaining four Diesels were more than the road needed. The two earliest, Nos. 70 and 80, were sold in 1959 to Republic Steel for use as switchers at Canton, Ohio.

In November 1959 J. B. Nance resigned the presidency of the railroad to take a position with the Martin Aircraft Company. He was replaced by one of the Ma & Pa's career employees, A. M. Bastress. Having joined the railroad in 1917 as a clerk in the ac-counting department, Bastress worked his way up to Traffic Man-ager. He had a very real fondness for the railroad and could be counted upon to preserve it, if anyone could.

Under the conditions of the late 1950's, preserving the Ma & Pa would take a bit of doing. The road lost $87,774 in 1958 and $48,380 in 1959. When the Red Lion Cabinet Company, which had provided about 58 per cent of the revenue in the Red Lion-Dallastown area, closed its plant, the Ma & Pa decided not to fight on. As late as 1956, this plant was responsible for about

Nos. 70 and 80, rather ordinary examples of Electro-Motive's art, both ply their trade currently at Republic Steel's Canton plant. *(Above, Bert Penny-packer; below, William S. Young)*

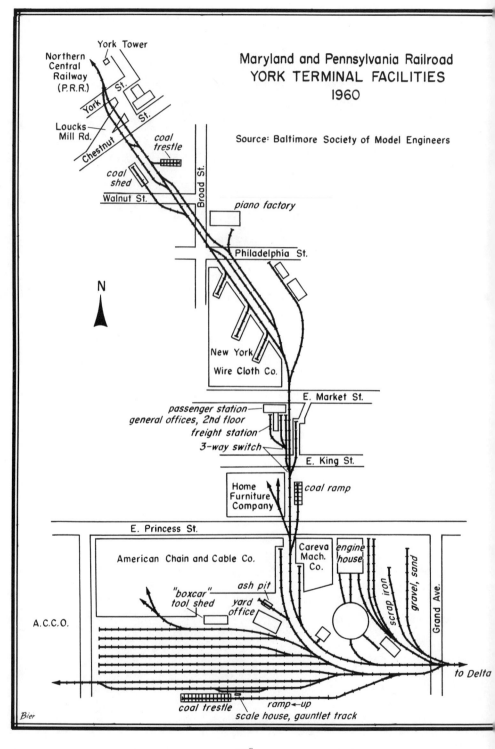

Maryland and Pennsylvania Railroad
YORK TERMINAL FACILITIES
1960

Source: Baltimore Society of Model Engineers

York Tower

Northern
Central
Railway
(P.R.R.)

York St.

Loucks
Mill Rd.

Chestnut St.

coal
trestle

coal
shed

Walnut St.

Broad St.

piano factory

Philadelphia St.

N

New York
Wire Cloth Co.

E. Market St.

passenger station
general offices, 2nd floor
freight station
3-way switch

E. King St.

Home
Furniture
Company

coal ramp

E. Princess St.

American Chain and Cable Co.

Careva
Mach.
Co.

engine
house

scrap iron

gravel, sand

Grand Ave.

"boxcar"
tool shed

ash pit

yard
office

A.C.C.O.

to Delta

Bier

coal trestle

ramp—up

scale house, gauntlet track

$120,000 in revenue. The railroad on October 15, 1959, applied to the ICC for total abandonment.

Unlike the dropping of the Maryland District, the proposed abandonment of the remaining line brought forth a substantial volume of opposition. The Funkhouser quarry, which had always been the line's principal shipper, had been sold in January 1959 to the Rubberoid Corporation, which state flatly that it wouldn't have bought the plant if it had expected a cessation of rail service, and predicted that it would have to shut down the operation. Similarly, the Maryland Green Marble Corporation, which operated the quarry at Whiteford, argued that its operation would be extremely difficult in absence of the railroad. Further, the Solite Company of Richmond, Virginia, testified that it planned to build a million dollar plant at Delta for the processing of slate from 50 acres of land it held locally. Solite proposed to produce a slate-based concrete about a third lighter than standard cement.

The Ma & Pa argued that, since the slate was sent out in granules and the marble mainly in terrazzo chips, it could be handled in trucks with no more difficulty than sand or cement.

The protestants' arguments swayed ICC Examiner Blond to recommend that the abandonment petition be denied. He believed that the railroad had prospects of further profitable operation, particularly if the Solite plant were built, and if Colonial Products opened the Red Lion Cabinet plant as it proposed to do. The ICC, accordingly, denied the petition in 1960 and directed the Ma & Pa to continue operation of the remaining line for a year.

President Bastress stated that he was not dismayed by the refusal. He argued that the year would give him time to try to dispose of the road to on-line shippers. There was little doubt that he would do whatever he could to keep the Ma & Pa running. Since the railroad had realized over $525,000 from the sale of the two locomotives and of the scrap from the south end, it was not short of cash and could continue deficit operations for some time.

Bastress inaugurated an austerity program, cutting maintenance sharply. The track was still in generally good shape, surely adequate for the Ma & Pa's 25-mile per hour speed limit. Weeds began to appear in ballast which, even in the depths of the depression, had been generally free of them. The trains kept running, however. The gross fell from $353,137 in 1959 to $309,582 in 1960, but the railroad reduced its loss to about $25,000.

In 1961 traffic picked up markedly. The railroad ran about three freights a week to Delta, and did switching every day in York. By the end of 1961, the railroad was covering its variable expenses by a small margin, and the prospects for survival were better than they had been for several years. Bastress, unfortunately, barely lived to see the improvement in the railroad's fortunes, for he died after a long illness, on September 28, 1961. Direction passed into the hands of another career employee of the railroad, Carl L. Amrein. An able operating man, Amrein was to superintend the Ma & Pa's shaky fortunes as General Manager. Shortly, he was also elected Vice-President. The presidency devolved upon the principal stockholder, Philip L. Poe of Baltimore. Already a man of 80, Poe was unlikely to be an active head of the railroad. Consequently, Amrein was assured of being the dominant figure in what remained of the Ma & Pa's independent history.

The prospect was not a bright one. Existing sources of traffic were demonstrably unable to support the railroad, and only the projected Solite plant at Delta appeared to offer any probability of significant additional tonnage. A second and a successful abandonment application seemed all but inevitable.

Events proved otherwise. The Solite plant was never built, but circumstances that the management could not have foreseen caused the Ma & Pa to survive and in greatly altered form even to prosper in the course of two additional decades.

MARYLAND & PENNSYLVANIA
RAILROAD COMPANY

1954-1955   No. 385

PASS   Mr. George W. Hilton

UNTIL DECEMBER 31ST, 1955   { UNLESS OTHERWISE ORDERED AND
                                 { SUBJECT TO CONDITIONS ON BACK

VALID WHEN COUNTERSIGNED BY
MYSELF OR E. J. WEBER
COUNTERSIGNED

E. J. Kelley   PRESIDENT

The prospect of discontinuance of passenger service on the Ma & Pa in 1954 brought relatively heavy loads for more than a week. Here is the last Saturday train on August 28, 1954, on the Gross trestle, photographed from locomotive 81 by fireman N. R. Young.

The Ma & Pa wound up passenger service on August 31, 1954, with this round trip of trains 1 and 2. Both gas-electrics plus a rented Pennsylvania Railroad coach handled the crowd. Above, locomotive 81, shown at Delta, handled the train north. Below, No. 70 is about to leave York with the train southbound. *(Both, N. R. Young)*

8

Emons Industries

Once the management had been denied abandonment in 1959, the railroad was essentially being operated involuntarily, but the officers made an honest effort to have it succeed. President Bastress met with the local shippers, who had organized to oppose the abandonment, and endeavored to work out traffic arrangements for the coming years. The shippers' association showed no interest in buying the railroad, but members promised to cooperate closely with the officers in endeavoring to make it viable. What such cooperation could accomplish was limited, however. The railroad's operating revenues came about 65 percent from the old Funkhouser quarry, now run by the Rubberoid Corporation. The rest, which came almost entirely from remaining plants in Red Lion and York, could not possibly support the railroad.

The railroad had a few things working for it. The management retained more than a half million in cash from the scrapping of the south end, sufficient to tide it over years of outright losses, and enough to provide an interest income of some $25,000 to put it in the black in better years. The 1960's proved to be the longest period of sustained prosperity in the country's history, with a large number of younger families and a vast amount of housing being built in suburban areas. The Ma & Pa had usually done well in such times. It was now at low enough ebb that survival, rather than prosperity, was the target, but the combination of circumstances did, at least, enable the railroad to last out the decade. In 1962 the company first reported what became its standard performance of the 1960's, losing a small amount of money on the rail operation, but ending slightly in the black because of interest income. In 1963 and 1964 it finished with small deficits, under $4,000 each year, but in 1965 it reported a net profit of $17,461.

Thereafter through 1970, the company remained in the black in spite of annual operating deficits.

Much as Baltimore's Catholic cathedral had given the last windfall of revenue to the southern district, expansion of a nuclear power station presented a totally unexpected source of traffic for the remaining mileage. In 1966 the Philadelphia Electric Company, attracted by a rural location and abundance of water, had built a pilot nuclear power station at Peach Bottom. The station was small enough that all of the construction materials had been brought in by truck. The power company was so pleased with performance of the plant that it decided upon expanding the facility with two large reactors. For this expansion the company brought in construction materials by rail. For the long run, it proposed to bring in approximately a carload of nuclear fuel per month and to ship out nuclear waste. Philadelphia Electric, to assure rail access to the plant, undertook to restore the old Peach Bottom branch which the Ma & Pa had abandoned in 1903. Construction began in November, 1968. The new line ran 3.5 miles from the terminus of the Ma & Pa at Slate Hill. The line generally followed the abandoned branch, but at a higher altitude and, surprisingly, with sharper curves. It opened on March 31, 1969, when No. 81 brought in five loaded boxcars. Revenues from the construction were important to the Ma & Pa in 1967, 1968 and 1969. Unfortunately for the railroad, a nuclear power station does not require any large volume of inputs and the fuel can be shipped safely by truck. Philadelphia Electric planned to use the line mainly for outbound shipments of radioactive waste to a point in South Carolina, but the company was never able to make an arrangement for this. The power company, which had built the line, retained title to the trackage, but contracted to pay the Ma & Pa a switching fee of $50,000 per year to operate it. This arrangement has been continued to the present in the apparent expectation that some agreement for rail movement of spent fuel to a dumping site can be arranged.

Traffic in connection with the building of the power plant was heavy enough to cause the Ma & Pa to buy in 1967 a third locomotive—a rebuilt Electro-Motive SC class switcher—from the Steelton & Highspire. Numbered 83, it joined 81 and 82 in mixed switching and road duty.

The mid-1960's saw a revival of passenger service on the Ma & Pa, though hardly on a common carrier basis. In 1964 and 1965 Byron Andrews operated some excursions with Ma & Pa Diesels and rolling stock. He bought a ten-wheeler from the Sumter & Choctaw Railway, but it proved impractical for the Ma & Pa. George Hart, a well known enthusiast in the Lancaster area, undertook to operate steam excursions in 1965. He ran trips from York to Yoe with former Canadian Pacific 4-6-2 1286, but the engine was too heavy for the trestles to the south. With Canadian Pacific 4-6-0 972 and Reading 0-6-0 1251 he managed with difficulty to run excursions all the way to Delta. Partly because the steam locomotives tended to spread the rails, the operation was discontinued in 1967. The railroad was becoming suitable for ten-mile-per-hour Diesel freight operation and little else.

Superfically, the Ma & Pa appeared to have made a come-back. The railroad had a net income of $25,235 in 1970, the best since the denial of the abandonment request. At this point, Philip L. Poe died on June 26, 1970. He was 91. Poe had been a pragmatic investment banker, in no sense an enthusiast who wanted to keep the Ma & Pa operating. In fact, he had begun his purchases of the railroad's stock in the 1950's with the expectation of eventually scrapping it. His death, however, was to raise the question of disposition of the majority of stock in the railroad. Poe's estate came into the hands of his son-in-law, Attorney H. Joel Barlow.

Presidency of the railroad devolved upon Carl Amrein. No man could have deserved the office more, for by 1970 he had literally devoted a lifetime to the Ma & Pa. As a teenager, he had gone to work as agent at the Fallston station on October 6, 1924. In 1927 he became dispatcher, but when the third trick dispatcher's job was abolished in 1935, he was reduced to a variety of clerical jobs. He had once been conductor during a strike. By 1942 he was chief clerk to the President, but in 1944 he became chief dispatcher. He became trainmaster in 1957, and rose to General Manager, Vice-President and Director quickly after 1961. Since he had worked up through the ranks—he had served in every major capacity except engineer—he was particularly gratified with the appointment. Congratulations came to him from presidents of several major railroads. An affable man with the courteous manner of a southern gentleman, his personality lent itself to the social

In the 1960s the Philadelphia Electric Company enlarged its Peach Bottom nuclear power station, causing about three years of non-recurring traffic to the Ma & Pa. In expectation of bringing in fuel and shipping out nuclear waste, Philadelphia Electric restored the Peach Bottom branch in 1969. The grade of the old branch, abandoned in 1903, was still visible behind the farmhouse, below, but the power company preferred to excavate a new and higher line over the same route. *(Philadelphia Electric Co.; Charles T. Mahan, Jr.)*

After 1971 operations on the Ma & Pa main line to Delta were of the character of No. 81 with two cars, above. As the photograph indicates, the track was in bad shape, so that operations were limited to 10 miles per hour. (M&PA)

The Ma & Pa's saviors proved to be men from the New York financial community, rather than from the railroad industry itself. Standing for their portrait are Emons Industries officials Vito J. Marino, Herman Lazarus, Robert Grossman, Harold Grossman, director Jerauld Wisbaum, Joseph Marino, and director William J. Peck. (Emons Industries)

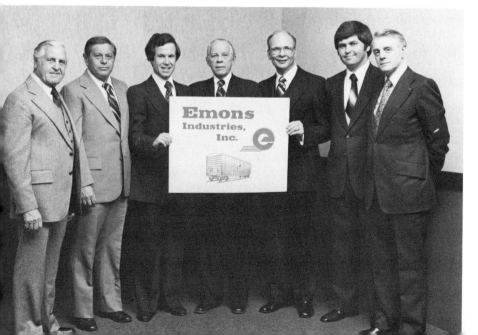

obligations of a railroad president.

Unfortunately, the Ma & Pa's fortunes turned for the worse shortly after Amrein assumed the presidency—for reasons which were beyond his control. The nuclear power station had stopped producing major revenue. In 1971 the Funkhouser quarry, now operated by the GAF Corporation, ceased operation. This would probably have been the ultimate disaster for the Ma & Pa. The source of some two thirds of operating revenue was gone, and nothing gave any prospect of replacing it. The remaining Green Marble quarry shipped only three or four cars a month, and because the output was in terrazzo chips, the traffic could readily move in trucks. As it proved, this traffic left the railroad by 1973. The Miller Chemical & Fertilizer Company at Whiteford, which received some inbound shipments, was the only other source of traffic in the Delta area. The Ma & Pa's management considered cutting the line back to Red Lion, but concluded that the traffic was too light to make the remnant viable. The railroad reported an operating deficit of $76,064.24 and a net deficit of $35,956.26 in 1971. Amrein was in favor of total abandonment, and there is little reason to doubt that the Interstate Commerce Commission would have acquiesced.

The Ma & Pa's survival was essentially due to a man who never played a formal role in the railroad's history. He was a New Jersey contractor and real estate man, Joseph C. Bonanno—unrelated to the alleged Mafia figure of similar name. Bonanno hit upon a plan of buying short line railroads to use as a base for circulation of boxcars in the general pool of freight cars of the American railroad system. He had already established working arrangements with the Cadillac & Lake City in Michigan and the LaSalle & Bureau County in Illinois. Later he acquired the Marianna & Blountstown in Florida. His practice was to buy used bad-order boxcars from trunk lines, upgrade them for interchange and let the railroad live on the *per diem* receipts. The Ma & Pa, or at minimum the York-Red Lion segment, might survive in this fashion.

Bonanno negotiated an option with Barlow to acquire the majority stock interest in the Ma & Pa. He began to search about for funds to effect the transaction. He might have succeeded, but he and his subsidiary corporations, Diversified Properties, Inc., and Magna Earth Enterprises, became embroiled in a legal action concerning transfer of some Penn Central boxcars to the LaSalle & Bureau County. Bonanno had a contract to buy from Equitable Life Assurance Society 466 boxcars which had been leased to the Penn Central. The cars were no longer fit for interchange. The Penn Central brought an action charging Bonanno with theft of serviceable boxcars as they arrived on the LaSalle & Bureau County. The short line was accused of having repainted them and sent them out as its own. Bonanno responded that the Penn Central had ineptly sent him the wrong cars. He was found free of wrongdoing, but required to pay $150,000 for having taken possession of serviceable equipment instead of bad-order boxcars.

Bonanno's troubles, though temporary, prevented his acquisition of the Ma & Pa. Among the groups which he approached in his efforts to finance the transaction was Amfre-Grant, Inc., a small conglomerate in the industrial fastener, hardware and exotic plant businesses. Amfre-Grant's officers, Harold Grossman, Robert Grossman, Joseph W. Marino, Vito J. Marino and Herman Lazarus, showed lively interest in Bonanno's idea. The firm bought Bonanno's car-owning subsidiary, Diversified Properties, and assumed Bonanno's option to buy control of the Ma & Pa. The conglomerate took over the Ma & Pa with a 70 percent stock interest on October 4, 1971, paying $100,000 in cash and $276,000 over a five-year period in 5 percent notes. Simultaneously Amfre-Grant changed its name to Emons Industries, Inc., the name of its previous subsidiary in the industrial fastener business. Emons sold off the fastener enterprise in June 1973, and the floral business in March 1976. Meanwhile, it was to expand wondrously in the railroad business. In April 1976 Emons moved its headquarters from New York to the Ma & Pa's station in York.

Emons Industries' principal interest in the Ma & Pa from the outset was entry into the North American freight car pool, but it never intended to use the railroad simply as a tax dodge. Rather, it wanted to prosper both as a car supplier and as a railroad. Consequently, the firm proceeded with expansion of both segments of the business.

Inevitably, the car supply business was to be the more important. Emons began its car operations simply, by taking the existing bad-order boxcars that Bonanno had bought, making heavy

Emons Industries' first venture in car supply was simply taking bad-order boxcars, mainly former Penn Central equipment, and restoring them to good order. The operation was performed out-of-doors in the York yard. (M&PA)

Emons Industries' second stage was rebuilding boxcars with new sides, roofs, brakes and safety fittings. These two views show the operation in progress, also out-of-doors at York, in 1976. (M&PA)

In 1977 Emons Industries built its own car shop on the York terminal property and began producing its own boxcars. The operation is highly professional. *(Emons Industries)*

No. 82 pulled 7500 out of the York carbuilding shop, the first of Emons Industries' fleet of new boxcars for interchange. Emons continued to use an adaptation of the traditional star herald of the Ma & Pa. *(Emons Industries)*

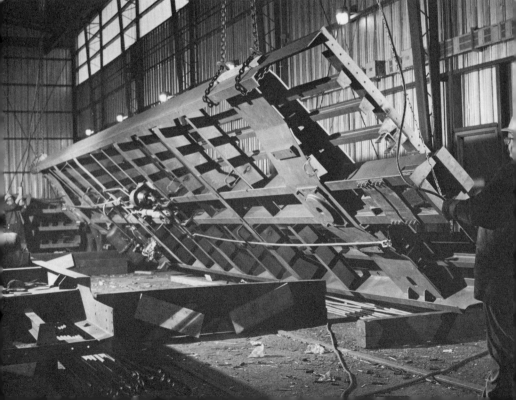

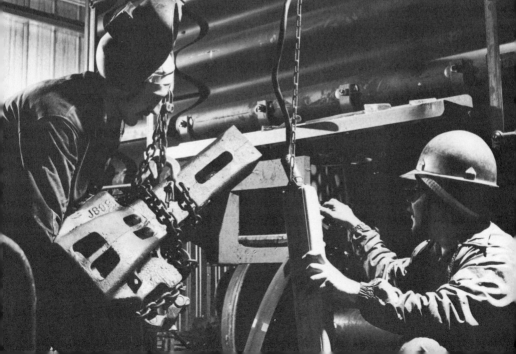

repairs and restoring them to service with Ma & Pa lettering. In some cases the cars were not even repainted. The entire operation was carried on out-of-doors in the York yards. The cars were spotted for on-line shippers and sent forth to earn *per diem*.

By 1973 the operation had progressed to the point that Emons began major rebuilding of cars. The company bought boxcars from the Penn Central, Chicago & Illinois Midland, Rio Grande and others for rebuilding with roller bearings; lengthening from 40 to 50 feet; addition of safety appliances and new brake equipment and replacement of roofs and similar major modifications. Once again the effort prospered. Boxcars bearing the Ma & Pa carload report marks, which had disappeared from the railroads in 1937 because of more stringent interchange requirements, were becoming common all over the nation. By early 1977 the company had decided to build a car shop with overhead cranes and modern facilities for carbuilding at York.

The new shop, which opened in November 1977, made possible building boxcars from scratch—the inevitable third stage of the operation. The company adopted a standard 50-foot, 70-ton boxcar design and turned out the first numbers in 1978. The shop is capable of producing three cars per eight-hour shift. At this rate the car fleet has grown rapidly. By mid-1980 it is expected to reach 3,700, not all of which are in Ma & Pa livery. Approximately 30 percent of the fleet is in free-running service, 35 percent assigned to specific shippers and 35 percent leased out. About 1,300 are owned by Emons, but lettered for the Waterloo Railroad, Columbus & Greenville, Patapsco & Back Rivers, Philadelphia Bethlehem & New England, and South Buffalo Railway. The geographical diversity has the incidental advantage of mitigating the Ma & Pa's traditional dependence on the eastern railroads. The first departure from boxcars took place in 1980 when Emons took delivery of 500 gondolas, 400 of which went to Bethlehem Steel's subsidiary railroads. Emons next plans to expand into covered hoppers for grain, open hoppers for coal and bulkhead flat cars. Emons has considered containerized equipment, but it has done nothing as yet to implement the idea.

Since 1978 *per diem* has been calculated on an hourly basis with a mileage component, in effect raising the daily *per diem* revenue from a car by about 30 percent. The change, together with incentive elements in *per diem* since 1970, brought about a billion dollars in capital to the car supply industry. The price of a plain 50-foot boxcar has risen from about $17,000 in 1974 to $40,000 in 1980; but Emons considers itself in a growth industry. It is not the largest firm in the industry, but appears to be among the most solidly financed. The company's net worth has reached $22 million and financial arrangements in progress should raise the figure to $27 million shortly.

Inevitably, the Ma & Pa has become a rather small part of Emons' operations, but the company has followed its original intention of taking railroading seriously. The railroad, which maintains its separate corporate identity, remained in the red through 1972, but beginning in 1973, reported positive net income because of the *per diem* earnings. Had Emons been interested only in car supply, the situation would probably have been a satisfactory one. The planning process whereby the Penn Central was amalgamated with smaller, bankrupt eastern railroads into the Conrail system provided the opportunity for a big expansion of the rail operation. The Pennsylvania had a branch from York southwest to Frederick, Maryland. Most of the traffic had been concentrated on the 18.5 miles from York to Hanover. Tropical storm Agnes of 1972—in point of dollar losses, the greatest natural disaster ever to hit America—had destroyed the bridge over the Monocacy River into Frederick, reducing the rest of the branch to small-town originations and terminations. In the planning of Conrail, this branch was not included. Emons believed the portion to Hanover was worth having, both for its on-line traffic and for its interchanges with the Western Maryland, part of the Chessie System. The Emons management was well aware that the Ma & Pa's single interchange with the Pennsylvania and its successors in York was a serious handicap, for the Chessie and Norfolk & Western systems were doing quite a bit better. The Hanover line would give the Ma & Pa access to the Chessie System both in York and Hanover.

Agnes had also knocked out the Pennsylvania's bridge over Codorus Creek just south of York on the old Northern Central main line to Baltimore. Since this had been mainly a line for long-gone passenger trains, and the freight was moving between Harrisburg and Baltimore by the electrified line on the east bank of the Susquehanna, the planners of Conrail had no intention of restoring the Northern Central. On the south side of York, however, the line served several industrial firms, which gave the prospect of profitable switching operations.

The Ma & Pa's current roster of six Diesel locomotives is serviced at the York enginehouse. Emons Industries adopted a school-bus yellow livery for safety reasons. (M&PA)

The Ma & Pa's Central Branch to Hyde includes the Pennsylvania Railroad's short stretch of street running in York. No. 81 is switching at the St. Regis Paper Company to the south. (M&PA)

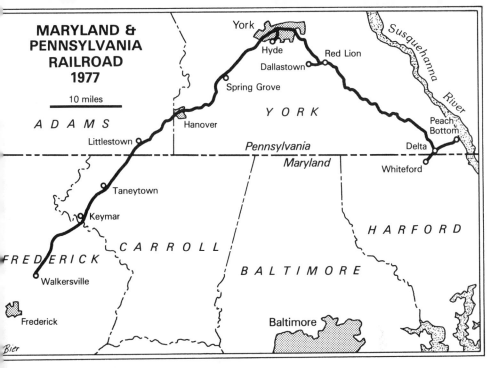

**MARYLAND &
PENNSYLVANIA
RAILROAD
1977**

10 miles

York
Hyde
Red Lion
Dallastown
Spring Grove

Y O R K

A D A M S
Hanover
Peach
Bottom

Littlestown
Delta

Pennsylvania
Maryland
Whiteford

Taneytown

Keymar

H A R F O R D

C A R R O L L

FRED ERICK

B A L T I M O R E

Walkersville

Frederick

Baltimore

Bier

Susquehanna River

On March 31, 1978, No. 86 took the last run on the former Pennsylvania Railroad line to Walkersville, Maryland. The final train is shown at Taneytown. The heavy deterioration of the track is evident. *(N. R. Young)*

The Keystone Distributing Company's huge warehouse is a major source of traffic on the Western Branch. (*N. R. Young*)

Trains on the traditional Ma & Pa main line are now switching movements of about a half dozen cars from York to Dallastown and Red Lion. (*Carl Amrein collection*)

Consequently, in the reformation of the Penn Central into Conrail, Emons, in the name of the Ma & Pa, bought the York-Hanover line and the former Northern Central as far as Hyde, Pennsylvania, about three miles south of York. The price was $250,000. The Ma & Pa was still a short line, but it was now the principal switching line in York and a facility for over 100 shippers. Carloadings would range from 2,400 to 3,000 per year, depending on the level of business activity, but, in any event, sufficient to allow the growing boxcar fleet to be sent forth in interchange.

The Railroad Reorganization and Regulatory Reform Act of 1976, which completed the Conrail reorganization, provided federal funds for operation of branch lines under state auspices. Pennsylvania and Maryland decided to continue running what was left of the Frederick branch, with the Ma & Pa as the designated operator. Emons had no illusions that this trackage could be profitable, and had shown no interest in buying it. The company was willing to operate the line under subsidy, and beginning April 1, 1976, simultaneously with taking over the Hanover and Hyde lines, began operating the Frederick branch as far as Walkersville, the last town short of the collapsed Monocacy River bridge. The Hanover and Hyde lines increased the Ma & Pa's mileage to 61 and the Walkersville operation added 30 more.

The expansion required additional motive power. The company went into the secondhand Diesel market to buy three more Electro-Motive units, an SW-9, an NW-2, and a GP-7, numbered 84 through 86, respectively. Nos. 84 and 86 were capable of operating in multiple unit with one another. By ordinary standards of the industry, No. 86 was the first actual road Diesel that the Ma & Pa ever had. Typically, it operated the runs to Walkersville.

While Emons was extending the railroad to the west, the traditional trackage of the Ma & Pa to the east was shrinking. Because of closure of the Funkhouser quarry and the Philadelphia Electric Company's inability to ship out nuclear wastes, operations to Delta amounted to a train or two per week, usually of only one or two cars. There was little incentive to maintain the line under the circumstances, and the track quickly became too deteriorated for operation. On June 14, 1978, the railroad declared a 60,000-pound weight limitation on the line beyond Red Lion. Since this was only about a quarter of the weight of any of the Diesel units, the order amounted to an absolute embargo on the old Ma & Pa main line. Because of the high water content of the soil along Muddy Creek, plants grow rapidly, so that the line was quickly covered with trees and brush, rendering it inoperable without a major clearing effort.

Nonetheless, Philadelphia Electric retained an interest in the line as an access facility to the power plant. In 1976 the power company and railroad drew up an agreement whereby Emons would sell the entire Ma & Pa main line between the Conrail interchange in York and Delta to Philadelphia Electric for $1. Emons would retain the yard and shop facilities in York. The power company would then restore the line to operable condition, straighten out some of the curves and otherwise modernize it. Philadelphia Electric would then lease it back to the Ma & Pa in perpetuity for $1 per year, plus a sliding scale of payments up to $20,000 per year, depending on the line's earnings. The quarries at Delta may reopen, and a plan for disposal of Philadelphia's garbage in abandoned quarries, which local residents have successfully resisted, may yet be carried out. Philadelphia Electric's inability to arrange a disposal site for its nuclear waste has prevented the agreement from being implemented. The project was estimated to cost Philadelphia Electric between $7 million and $9 million in 1976, but probably would run double that in the 1980's. If the agreement is not carried out, there seems little prospect of the line beyond Red Lion surviving.

In 1978 the State of Maryland lost its enthusiasm for operation of the former Frederick branch. The traffic was meager, and the line was in such bad shape that derailments were continual. The subsidy was withdrawn and on March 31, 1978, the Ma & Pa gave up operation south of the state line.* Pennsylvania was willing to continue the subsidy to operate as far as Littlestown, six miles beyond Hanover and just short of the border. Currently, the subsidy amounts to $32,000 per year. This proves a favorable arrangement for the railroad, since Littlestown has three shippers, a cabinet factory, a metal works and a foundry that generate three or four cars a week.

---

*At the present writing in early 1980, a new short line, the Maryland Midland Railway, has been organized to operate the Taneytown-Walkersville trackage.

As the railroad is operated in 1980, the former Ma & Pa line to Red Lion, including the Dallastown spur, is considered the Eastern Branch. Trains of mainly five or six cars operate twice a week. The Colonial Division of Wickes Corporation ships on Conrail partly completed cabinets to other plants of the firm. The Flinchbaugh Corporation at Red Lion is a defense contractor which ships projectiles. Some lumber moves into furniture factories in the town. The Dallastown branch survives on inbound movements of steel and aluminum to Gischner Mobile Systems, a manufacturer of trailers. Unfortunately, all of this combined would not come close to supporting the line in absence of the other rail operations and the car supply business. Emons has no plans to abandon the line, however. In fact, Emons would like to develop an industrial park on the site of the United Piece Die Works in York, and also to develop the former Allen farm on the line between York and Red Lion.

The newly-acquired rail lines are considerably more robust. The Hanover line, which is known as the Western Branch, has several major shippers or consignees. The Keystone Distributing Company is one of the largest food wholesalers in the area, a continual source of inbound movements. The firm of Bowen-McLaughlin at Bair ships out over 200 cars per year. The Glatfelter Paper Company maintains a plant at Spring Grove, the principal intermediate town, and a warehouse on the west side of York. The Red Rose Feed division of Carnation and National Gypsum also have major plants on the Western Branch. Traffic warrants trains averaging about six cars five days a week, usually pulled by the GP-7, No. 86.

The remnant of the Northern Central line which Emons had acquired became the Central Branch of the Ma & Pa. The line, though it barely gets out of York, serves several industrial plants, including a major installation of the St. Regis Paper Company. The traffic warrants a train of three to six cars five or six days a week. This line has some additional traffic potential. The Stewartstown Railroad, which was isolated by the closure of the Northern Central line, would like to resume operations by restoring the bridge over Codorus Creek, plus two smaller ones that Agnes also knocked out. The Stewartstown could then reopen its own line and operate the Northern Central from New Freedom to Hyde.

Of the three railroad divisions of the present Ma & Pa, the Western and Central branches each produce about 45 percent of the revenue and would be viable as a shortline railroad. The Eastern Branch, the former Ma & Pa to Red Lion and Dallastown, amounts to about ten percent of the revenue and would not be viable independently. It is not surprising that only the Eastern Branch presents any difficult operating problems. The entire railroad operation amounts to less than 5 percent of Emons' revenues, but owing to the growth of the car supply operation, even that percentage is shrinking. Thus, the surviving portion of the former Ma & Pa amounts to only about half of one percent of the income of the conglomerate in which it now finds itself.

In spite of the small percentage of Emons' revenues which the railroad represents, the rail lines are run very professionally. Since members of Emons' management had their background in the New York financial community, they professed no professional competence in railroading. They hired as their Vice-President and General Manager William J. Partington, a career New York Central railroader. Partington had risen from carman on the Central to Supervisor of Cars for the Northern District in Detroit, and finally, to Supervisor of Car Utilization for the entire railroad in the general offices in New York. After the merger he became Manager of Car Utilization in the Projects and Planning Department of the Penn Central in Philadelphia. He had particularly identified himself with computerization of car supply. In all, he had 14 years in mechanical departments and eight in transportation, almost all concerned with car service. The attractions of this background were obvious to Emons when it hired him in 1975.

The Ma & Pa's current operations are short enough that it operates basically as a switching line. The railroad operates under short line rules, which allow cutting crews to three men from the four or five which the Penn Central had used. Cabooses have been discontinued. Emons installed 25-watt radios on the locomotives and equipped conductors, brakemen, maintenance-of-way people and all supervisors with walkie-talkies. Train orders are issued for movements on the Eastern and Western Branches, but the Central Branch is within the York yard limits. The railroad calls four or five crews per day. Normally, five locomotives are available and one is down for heavy repairs. The former Pennsylvania Railroad lines were in very bad shape, so Emons has had to put in over

4,500 ties. No very high standards of right-of-way are striven for. It is a 10-mile-per-hour railroad, but even this is an improvement over the 8-mile-per-hour speed limit the Federal Railroad Administration had slapped on the Penn Central's Hanover line.

Since the Ma & Pa has become the dominant switching line in York, Emons has had talks with Conrail about taking over the remainder of the city's switching operations, but Conrail has shown no interest. The Ma & Pa's interchange is currently about 65 percent with Conrail and 35 percent with the Chessie System, with the latter expanding.

Formally, the Ma & Pa has retained its corporate identity within Emons and will apparently continue to do so. Amrein continued as President until 1973 when he retired, just short of 50 years of service to the railroad. He has remained as Director, and Emons draws on his impressive knowledge continually. His replacement was Herman Lazarus of Emons. When Lazarus retired in 1980, he was replaced by Joseph Marino. Partington operated the railroad until April 1980, when he left the firm.

Emons took control of the railroad by buying 70 percent of its stock. For tax reasons the incentive to bring the holdings to over 80 percent was very considerable. By a tender offer at $22 per share—and later at $200 per share—Emons managed to get its holdings up to 98.9 percent. The remaining 48 shareholders were then bought out on very favorable terms. After the ICC approved a reverse stock split, they were bought out for the equivalent of about $526 per share. The railroad then became a wholly-owned subsidiary of Emons. Since stock had sunk to about $1 per share at various times when the Ma & Pa was doing poorly, anyone who stuck with his interest did very well indeed.

And so it was that the Maryland & Pennsylvania Railroad survived as a corporate entity, beating odds that seemed insuperable. Had not it become the base for the present large car service supply, it would almost certainly have perished in 1971, or as shortly thereafter as the ICC granted permission. The remaining mileage from York to Dallastown and Red Lion appears to be in no immediate danger, and there is still some prospect of restoration of the line to Delta. In any real sense, however, the old Ma & Pa of No. 6, the *York Mail* and Funkhouser's quarry is gone forever. Like the models and memories, the modern boxcars that bear the familiar herald will serve to memorialize that beloved railroad.

Canadian Pacific No. 972 on Maryland & Pennsylvania turntable at York, Pa. Below, CP No. 972 on Ma & Pa, eastbound at High Rock, Pa. (*H. H. Harwood, Jr.*)

Ten-wheeler 972 hauls an excursion on the new Peach Bottom branch at Slate Hill. Below, the Canadian Pacific engine teams with Reading No. 1251 on a southbound excursion at Bridgeton. (*H. H. Harwood, Jr.*)

Reading No. 1251 stops at Yoe on a southbound fantrip. Below, Canadian Pacific No. 1286 passes Ore Valley en route to Yoe — the farthest point the big engine could reach on the Ma & Pa. (*H. H. Harwood, Jr.*)

Epilogue, 1999

When the second edition of this book appeared in 1980, little was left of the Maryland & Pennsylvania. The portion of the railroad from York to Red Lion survived unprofitably, along with the York terminal facilities. The corporate structure of the railroad had been used by a conglomerate, Emons Industries, as a vehicle for a car-building and car-leasing operation, but also to operate some former Pennsylvania Railroad trackage from York west to Hanover and beyond. The former Ma & Pa trackage east from York to the Red Lion area was not expected to survive—and it did not. The company applied to the Interstate Commerce Commission to abandon it in 1983; the rails and ties were sold to a scrap merchant on September 22, 1986, and removed. In 1999 all that remains of the former Ma & Pa is the York yard and terminal, and about two-and-a-half miles running east as far as Mt. Rose Avenue, in York. Emons moved its office out of the old York station to a downtown location in 1982.

The former Pennsylvania trackage to the west of York was profitable and has remained so. The company still operates it, but only as far as Hanover. This trackage serves the railroad's biggest customer, P. H. Gladfelter & Co., in Spring Grove. This firm, which engages in cogeneration of electric power, receives unit trains of coal of up to 110 cars. Emons also acquired the former Western Maryland Railway entry into York, and operates it as Yorkrail, Inc. This presents a problem in the assignment of crews, for the Ma & Pa is a unionized operation and Yorkrail is not. Yorkrail crosses the Ma & Pa at Spring Grove, and also brings cargo into Gladfelter. The Maryland & Pennsylvania also operates two-and-a-half miles of the former Pennsylvania Railroad Northern Central line south from York to Hyde.

The car-building and -leasing operation of Emons has not survived. It was one of several such operations brought forth by a federal policy intended to deal with periodic shortages of boxcars. The shortages were actually produced by the way cars were priced. Railroads paid for the use of one another's cars by a fee collusively set through the *per diem* agreement. This was not a market-determined price, and it did not vary to deal with short-run fluctuations in demand. Worse, this system of pricing insulated the technology of individual boxcars from market forces that were widely expected, in a deregulated environment, to phase it out in favor of a containerized technology. The deregulated environment took shape in the form of the Staggers Rail Act of 1980 under the Carter administration and the abolition of the Interstate Commerce Commission under the Clinton administration. Emons' car building ended in 1981, and its car-leasing operation in 1991. The car-building shop was converted, first, to a repair facility and then to an intermodal transfer—a move consistent with the widespread expectation that deregulation would accelerate intermodalism.

Emons Industries went bankrupt and was reorganized in 1986 as Emons Transportation Group, Inc., of which Emons Industries became an inactive subsidiary. The new Emons expanded into operation a total of seven short lines in eastern Pennsylvania. It made its biggest acquisition, the American trackage of the Atlantic & St. Lawrence, the former Grand Trunk line to Portland, Maine, in May, 1989. In December, 1998, it acquired the Quebec portion of the same railway from the Canadian National, which gave it a through route of 259 miles from Sainte Rosalie on the CN main line east of Montreal to Portland.

Emons acquired in the name of the Maryland & Pennsylvania three additional locomotives in 1988, Electro-Motive GP-7 units similar to 86. They were purchased from Rail Systems, Inc., and numbered 1500, 1502, and 1504. All were secondhand units, reportedly the former Santa Fe 2417, 2426, and 2425, respectively. Locomotive 81 was sold to Gladfelter, which has donated it to the Strasburg Railroad, where it is a static exhibit.

Emons believes it has benefited from the deregulation of the railroad industry, and it anticipates benefiting from the division of Conrail between the Norfolk Southern and the CSX Corporation—an action pending at the present writing in early 1999. The Maryland & Pennsylvania will have access to both CSX and the Norfolk Southern directly, and also to the Canadian Pacific system, which will reach York via trackage rights on the Northern Central line.

The railroad has given rise to two historical societies. The Maryland & Pennsylvania Railroad Preservation & Historical Society (P.O. Box 224, Spring Grove, PA 17352) engages in archival preservation and publishes a quarterly magazine, *Timetable*. The Maryland & Pennsylvania Preservation Society (P.O. Box 5122, York, PA 17405) is principally devoted to an effort to preserve and restore to operation a portion of the line in Pennsylvania. It owns track from the Muddy Creek Forks to Laurel, which it operates with an 18-ton Plymouth gasoline locomotive, publishes a quarterly newsletter, *York Mail,* and is restoring a Jackson & Sharp coach similar to Ma & Pa 2125.

My thanks are due to Robert Grossman of Emons Transportation for the information to update the account of Emons since 1980. Stewart Rhine and Jean Sansonetti provided me with information on the two historical societies. Thanks, not for the first time, go to Charles T. Mahan Jr., for furnishing me with a print of his photograph of 62 on the Stirrup Run trestle for use on the cover. I appreciated the quick agreement of the Johns Hopkins University Press production staff with my view of many years that this is the best single photograph ever taken of the day-to-day operation of the railroad.

Appendixes

Maryland & Pennsylvania Railroad Company

TIME-TABLE No. 61

IN EFFECT

SUNDAY, APRIL 30, 1950

AT 12.01 O'CLOCK A. M.
EASTERN STANDARD TIME.

FOR THE INFORMATION AND GOVERNMENT OF EMPLOYES ONLY.

THIS COMPANY RESERVES THE RIGHT TO VARY FROM IT AT PLEASURE.

J. B. NANCE,	C. L. AMREIN,	R. O. PICKING,
President & General Manager.	Chief Dispatcher.	Trainmaster.

MARYLAND DISTRICT—BALTIMORE AND DELTA

NORTHBOUND — TIME TABLE No. 61 — SOUTHBOUND

APRIL 30, 1950

Third Class 31 — Daily Except Sunday	First Class .7 — Daily Except Sunday	First Class 3 — Daily Except Sunday	Distance from Baltimore	Station Number	STATIONS	Telegraph Call	Distance from York	First Class 8 — Daily Except Sunday	First Class 12 — Daily Except Sunday	Third Class 32 — Daily Except Sunday
A. M.	P. M.	A. M.			LEAVE — ARRIVE			A. M.	P. M.	P. M.
5 00	1 50	7 10	...	0	W........BALTIMORE......TD	X	77.2	10 35	5 20	12 55
					2.6					
5 07	f 1 57	f 7 17	2.6	3	........EVERGREEN.........		74.6	f 10 23	f 5 06	12 46
					0.6					
5 09	f 2 00	f 7 20	3.2	3B	....NOTRE DAME......		74.0	f 10 21	f 5 04	12 44
					1.1					
5 13	f 2 04	f 7 24	4.3	4	........HOMELAND........T		72.9	f 10 18	f 5 01	12 39
					0.8					
5 15	f 2 06	f 7 26	5.1	5	........WOODBROOK........T		72.1	f 10 16	f 4 59	12 36
5 18	f 2 08	f 7 28	6.2	6	........SHEPPARD........T		71.0	f 10 14	f 4 57	12 33
					0.8					
5 21	s 2 14	s 7 35	7.0	7	........TOWSON........TD	SN	70.2	s 10 12	s 4 55	12 30
					0.7					
5 24	f 2 17	f 7 38	7.7	8	.... TOWSON HEIGHTS ....T		69.5	f 10 04	f 4 43	12 27
					1.9					
5 32	f 2 21	f 7 42	9.6	10	........OAKLEIGH..........		67.6	f 9 59	f 4 38	12 20
					1.6					
5 40	f 2 25	s 7 46	11.2	11	........LOCH RAVEN......T		66.0	f 9 55	s 4 34	12 14
					0.7					
5 48	f 2 26	f 7 47	11.9	12B	W..MARYLAND SCHOOL....		65.3	f 9 53	f 4 32	12 09
					0.7					
5 50	f 2 27	f 7 48	12.6	13A	........SUMMERFIELD........T		64.6	f 9 52	f 4 31	12 04
					0.8					
5 53	f 2 29	f 7 50	13.4	13	........NOTCH CLIFF..........		63.8	f 9 50	f 4 29	12 01
					1.1					
5 57	s 2 34	s 7 56	14.5	15	........GLENARM........TD	GN	62.7	s 9 48	s 4 27	11 57
					1.3					
6 01	f 2 38	f 8 00	15.8	16	........LONG GREEN......T		61.4	f 9 43	f 4 23	11 50
					1.0					
6 05	s 2 41	s 8 03	16.8	17	........HYDE........T		60.4	s 9 40	s 4 20	11 45
					0.9					
6 08	2 43	8 05	17.7	18A	..RUTLEDGE'S SIDING....		59.5	9 38	4 18	11 42
					0.7					
6 10	s 2 45	s 8 07	18.4	18	........BALDWIN........T		58.8	s 9 37	s 4 17	11 40
					1.9					
6 22	2 48	8 10	20.3	20	...LITTLE GUNPOWDER.T		56.9	9 31	4 11	11 25
					0.9					
6 26	f 2 51	f 8 13	21.2	21	........LAUREL BROOK........		56.0	f 9 29	f 4 09	11 20
					1.1					
6 33	s 2 56	s 8 19	22.3	22	........FALLSTON........T		54.9	s 9 26	s 4 06	11 15
					1.9					
6 43	f 3 01	f 8 23	24.2	24	W........VALE........T		53.0	f 9 20	f 4 00	11 00
					2.3					
7 05	s 3 12	s 8 35	26.5	27	........BEL AIR........TD	KN	50.7	s 9 15	s 3 55	10 45
					2.0					
7 11	f 3 17	f 8 40	28.5	29	........BYNUM........T		48.7	f 9 05	f 3 45	10 00
					1.8					
7 20	s 3 23	s 8 46	30.3	30	........FOREST HILL........T		46.9	s 9 01	s 3 41	9 46
					2.0					
7 30	f 3 28	f 8 51	32.3	32	........SHARON..........		44.9	f 8 53	f 3 32	9 25
					0.5					
7 33	3 31^{12}	8 52^{8}	32.8	32A	HORNBERGER'S SIDING T		44.4	8 52^{3}	3 31^{7}	9 22
					0.9					
7 37	f 3 33	f 8 54	33.7	34	........FERNCLIFF..........		43.5	f 8 49	f 3 29	9 20
					1.6					
7 47	s 3 38	s 9 00	35.3	35	W..........ROCKS..........		41.9	s 8 45	s 3 25	9 14
					2.0					
8 09	f 3 46	f 9 08^{32}	37.3	37	........MINEFIELD........T		39.9	f 8 39	f 3 19	9 08
					1.3					
8 14	s 3 50	s 9 12	38.6	39	........STREET........T		38.6	s 8 36	s 3 16	8 50
					1.7					
8 19	s 3 54	s 9 16	40.3	40	........PYLESVILLE........T		36.9	s 8 31	s 3 11	8 40
					2.1					
8 26$^{8}_{32}$	s 4 00	s 9 22	42.4	42	........WHITEFORD......TD	WD	34.8	s 8 26$^{31}_{32}$	s 3 06	8 26
					0.9					
8 30	s 4 03	s 9 25	43.3	43	........CARDIFF..........		33.9	s 8 22	s 3 02	8 10
					0.5					
9 05	s 4 07	s 9 30	43.8	44	........DELTA........TD	RH	33.4	s 8 20	s 3 00	8 00
A. M.	P. M.	A. M.			ARRIVE — LEAVE			A. M.	P. M.	A. M.
4 05	2 17	2 20			Time Over District			2 15	2 20	4 55

TIME TABLE No. 61

APRIL 30, 1950

NORTHBOUND Third Class 31 Daily Except Sunday	First Class 7 Daily Except Sunday	First Class 3 Daily Except Sunday	Distance from Baltimore	Station Number	STATIONS	Telegraph Call	Distance from York	SOUTHBOUND First Class 8 Daily Except Sunday	First Class 12 Daily Except Sunday	Third Class 32 Daily Except Sunday
A.M.	P.M.	A.M.			LEAVE .... ARRIVE			A.M.	P.M.	A.M.
9 05	s 4 07	s 9 30	43.8	44	.............DELTA.............TD (2.1)	RH	33.4	s 8 20	s 3 00	8 00
9 15	f 4 12	f 9 35	45.9	46	........BRYANSVILLE......T (1.0)		31.3	f 8 10	f 2 50	6 50
9 20	f 4 15	f 9 38	46.9	47	.........CASTLE FIN.........T (2.5)		30.3	f 8 07	f 2 47	6 45
9 32	f 4 21	f 9 44	49.4	49	........SOUTHSIDE........T (1.2)		27.8	f 8 01	f 2 41	6 35
9 45	s 4 25	s 9 48	50.6	51	.....WOODBINE.........T (1.0)		26.6	s 7 57	s 2 37	6 25
9 50	s 4 28	s 9 51	51.6	52	.........BRIDGETON.........T (1.9)		25.6	s 7 54	s 2 34	6 20
9 56³	f 4 33	f 9 56³¹	53.5	54	.... BRUCE.............T (3.0)		23.7	f 7 49	f 2 29	6 15
10 20	s 4 40	s 10 03	56.5	56	.MUDDY CREEK FORKS.TD (0.6)	MC	20.7	s 7 42	s 2 22	6 05
10 25	s 4 43	s 10 06	57.1	57	.........HIGH ROCK......... (2.0)		20.1	s 7 39	s 2 19	6 00
10 41	4 48	10 11	59.1	59A	LAUREL PASSING SIDING (0.3)		18.1	7 34	2 14	5 53
10 52	s 4 49	s 10 12	59.4	59	.........LAUREL.........T (1.5)		17.8	s 7 33	s 2 13	5 52
10 56	f 4 53	f 10 16	60.9	61A	.........FENMORE......... (0.4)		16.3	f 7 29	f 2 09	5 47
10 58	s 4 55	s 10 18	61.3	61	.........BROGUEVILLE......T (2.3)		15.9	s 7 28	s 2 08	5 43
11 10	s 5 01	s 10 24	63.6	64	.........FELTON.........TD (1.2)	FN	13.6	s 7 22	s 2 02	5 33
11 20	f 5 04	f 10 27	64.8	65	.........BROWNTON.. ......T (2.0)		12.4	f 7 17	f 1 57	5 25
11 32	f 5 09	f 10 32	66.8	67	.........SPRINGVALE......... (1.5)		10.4	f 7 13	f 1 53	5 20
11 50	s 5 16	s 10 42	68.3	68	.........RED LION.........TD (1.0)	RN	8.9	s 7 10	s 1 50	5 15
11 55	5 18	10 44	69.3	69	DALLASTOWN JUNCT'N T (1.2)		7.9	6 59	1 41	4 45
12 00	s 5 24	s 10 49	70.5	B 2	.........DALLASTOWN......T (1.2)		9.1	s 6 58	s 1 38	4 40
12 05	5 28	10 53	69.3	69	DALLASTOWN JUNCT'N T (0.5)		7.9	6 52	1 32	4 30
12 10	s 5 32	s 10 57	70.3	70	.............YOE............. (0.5)		6.9	s 6 48	s 1 28	4 25
12 14	f 5 33	f 10 58	70.8	71	............RELAY............ (1.3)		6.4	f 6 46	f 1 26	4 20
12 19	f 5 36	f 11 01	72.1	72	.........ORE VALLEY......... (0.7)		5.1	f 6 43	f 1 23	4 15
12 23	f 5 37	f 11 02	72.8	73A	.............BEN ROY............. (0.5)		4.4	f 6 41	f 1 21	4 13
12 28	f 5 38	f 11 03	73.3	73	.........ENTERPRISE......... (1.1)		3.9	f 6 40	f 1 20	4 12
12 33	f 5 40	f 11 05	74.4	74	.........PAPER MILL......... (0.9)		2.8	f 6 38	f 1 18	4 08
12 38	f 5 42	f 11 07	75.3	75	.........PLANK ROAD......... (1.9)		1.9	f 6 36	f 1 16	4 05
12 50	5 55	11 20	77.2	77	W.............YORK.........TD	K		6 30	1 10	4 00
P.M.	P.M.	A.M.			ARRIVE .... LEAVE			A.M.	P.M.	A.M.
3 45	1 48	1 50			Time Over District			1 50	1 50	4 00

"W" indicates Water Station. In addition to those shown, Water Stations are located at or near Mile Posts 48 and 66.
"T" indicates Telephone Station. "D" indicates Telegraph Station.

SPECIAL INSTRUCTIONS.

ALL SOUTHBOUND trains will have absolute right over trains of the same class running in the opposite direction.

Rule 19 is hereby amended by adding thereto a sentence reading as follows: "Marker lamps (not lighted) may be used by day in lieu of green flags."

Rule 92 is hereby changed by the cancellation of the first sentence contained therein, making the complete rule as revised read: "92. A train must not leave a station in advance of its schedule leaving time."

The attention of Conductors and Enginemen of trains not having the right of track is directed to Rule No. 83.

All trains must obtain Clearance Form A before leaving Baltimore or York.

All trains and engines reduce speed to ten (10) miles per hour over all road or street crossings in Baltimore City limits (Homeland to North Avenue, inclusive).

Attention of Engineers is called to Bulletin No. 292 of June 22, 1922, regarding use of whistle in Baltimore City limits.

All locomotives and steam trains will flag and all motor trains will be brought to a complete stop immediately before crossing the following streets in York:

Hill, Albemarle, Norway, Pattison, Girard Ave., Princess, King, Market, Philadelphia, Broad, Walnut and Chestnut.

On week-days, motor car piloted by Foreman of Section 8 has right between Relay and Plank Road over all Southbound extra trains for thirty minutes prior to the assigned quitting time of Section 8. All running orders for Southbound extra trains between Plank Road and Relay must contain the assigned quitting time of Section 8.

Towson Estates, Springwood Park, Hollywood, Norway and Girard will be flag stops for all passenger trains.

Schedule meeting or passing points are indicated on the Time Table by figures in *full-faced type.*

Standard clocks are located in the Chief Dispatcher's office, Baltimore, and in the Agent's office, York.

YARD LIMITS AND REGULATIONS.

YARD LIMITS.

Baltimore.—From Morgan Millwork Co. to a point ft. north of north switch at Homeland.

Delta-Whiteford.—From a point 800 ft. south of S Spur to Mile Post 44, including the Slate Hill branch.

Red Lion.—From a point 500 ft. south of south en passing siding to York County Chair Co. siding.

York.—From Mile Post 75 to P. R. R. Junction.

YARD REGULATIONS.

Except as noted below, all trains and engines mus run through yards with the utmost caution. Engine must observe that the switches are set right, look out signals, and keep a sharp lookout for trains ahead. T must invariably run expecting to find the track obstruc by trains ahead of them. Shifting engines may work main tracks in yards as extras without orders.

Exceptions.—Baltimore yard engine will not g north of Mile Post One (1) without clearance fror Dispatcher. Unless restricted by train order, a trains, both scheduled and extra, may run throug that part of Baltimore yard between north yar limit and Mile Post One (1) without regard to yar engines.

See instructions under "Special Instructions" in reg to street crossings in Baltimore and York Yard limits.

COMPANY SURGEONS.

Dr. F. J. Kirby, St. Joseph's Hospital, Baltimore, Mc
Dr. J. A. Hunt, Delta, Pa.
Dr. John F. Bacon, York, Pa.

On page 197, No. 42 works hard against the grade at Sheppard, Maryland with train number 31. On page 198, Nos. 41 and 43 pull number 32 southbound near Baldwin. *(Both, Charles T. Mahan, Jr.)*

LOCOMOTIVE ROSTERS*

NORTH END PREDECESSORS: MIDDLE DIVISION, PEACH BOTTOM RAILWAY—YORK & PEACH BOTTOM RAILWAY—YORK SOUTHERN RAILROAD. GAUGE: 3'-0".

Number	Wheel Arrangement	Builder	Builder's Number	Year Built	Drivers	Cylinders	Pressure	Tractive Effort	Total Weight	Name
1.	0-6-0	Porter-Bell	190	1874	30"	9½x14"			11 tons	Rufus Wiley
2.	2-4-0	Porter-Bell	205	1874	36"	10x16"			13½ tons	S. G. Boyd
3.	0-6-6t	Mason	561	1876	34"	12x16"			19 tons	
4.	2-6-0	Baldwin	4442	1878	36"	12x16"			19½ tons	
5.	2-6-0	Pittsburgh	624	1882	42½"	12x18"			20 tons	
6.	4-4-0	Pittsburgh	705	1884	43"	12x18"				

Notes: No. 1 is reported in the Porter-Bell builder's list and the 1889 Porter catalog as an 0-6-0, but the notes of C. B. Chaney indicate that it was a 2-4-0. The engine burst its boiler June 29, 1882, but was sold to a lumber company at Williamsport.

No. 3, a standard Mason bogie, was hard on track and derailed frequently. It was retired on the arrival of No. 4 in 1878.

Nos. 4, 5, and 6 became Baltimore & Lehigh 14, 15, and 16 upon the merger of 1891.

Maryland & Pennsylvania Nos. 1, 2, and 3 were originally owned by the York Southern. See M&PA roster below.

*The author has compiled these rosters mainly from the material in the C. B. Chaney collection in the Smithsonian Institution. Additional information has come from G. M. Best, Charles T. Mahan, Jr., Benjamin F. G. Kline, Jr., W. R. Hicks, Thomas Norrell, Prof. Sylvan R. Wood, Charles E. Fisher, Roy W. Carlson, John A. Rehor, Rev. Albert J. Wagner, Martin M. Flattley, Jr., H. L. Goldsmith, John Baskin Harper, the Illinois Central Railroad, the Nickel Plate Road, and the Republic Steel Company.

SOUTH END PREDECESSORS: BALTIMORE & DELTA RAILWAY – MARYLAND CENTRAL RAIL-
ROAD – BALTIMORE & LEHIGH RAILROAD. GAUGE: 3'-0'.

Number	Wheel Arrangement	Builder	Builder's Number	Year Built	Drivers	Cylinders	Total Weight	Name
1.	2-6-0	Brooks	596	1881	41"	14x18"	22½ tons	Enoch Pratt
2.	2-6-0	Baldwin (?)		1881(?)				John M. Dennison
3.	2-8-0	Baldwin	6134	1882	36"	15x20"	30 tons	Thomas C. Jenkins
4.	2-8-0	Baldwin	6140	1882	36"	15x20"	30 tons	George S. Brown
5.	4-4-0	Pittsburgh	707	1883	49"	15x20"	28 tons	
6.	4-4-0	Pittsburgh	708	1883	49"	15x20"	28 tons	
7.	4-4-0	Pittsburgh	949	1887	49"	15x20"	28 tons	
8.	4-4-0	Grant	1524	1882	46"	14x20"	24 tons	
9.	4-4-0	Grant	1525	1882	46"	14x20"	24 tons	
10.	2-6-0	Brooks	2411	1893	42"	15x20"		
11.	2-6-0	Hinkley (?)	1702(?)	1887				
12.	4-4-0	Hinkley	1582(?)	1882				
13.	4-4-0	Hinkley	1583(?)	1882				
14.	2-6-0	Ex-York & Peach Bottom 4, q. v.						
15.	2-6-0	Ex-York & Peach Bottom 5, q. v.						
16.	4-4-0	Ex-York & Peach Bottom 6, q. v.						

Notes: No. 2 is reported in the C. B. Chaney notes to have been a Baldwin engine, but it has not been identified in the builder's list.

Nos. 3 and 4 were built as Denver & Rio Grande 292-293, but diverted to the B&D on completion. No. 3 was sold to the Banner Lumber Company of Kentucky, and No. 4 was wrecked at Vale in 1899.

No. 5 was sold to the Newport & Sherman's Valley, where it also carried No. 5.

No. 6 was sold to the Tionesta Valley, where it was renumbered 8.

No. 7 was sold in 1900 to the Bellaire Zanesville & Cincinnati, where it was renumbered 11. On the successor Ohio River & Western, it was renumbered 9667 about 1918. It was withdrawn about 1928.

Nos. 8 and 9 were purchased secondhand by the B&L about 1892. Since no complete Grant builder's list has been discovered, it is not possible to identify definitely the original owner. C. B. Chaney believed them to be of a series on the Texas & St. Louis illustrated in chapter IV. Since Chaney's notes show some ambiguity between the T&StL and the Toledo Cincinnati & St. Louis, John A. Rehor suggests that the engines may have been part of a set of ten ordered by the TC&StL in June, 1882, possibly TC&StL 75-76.

No. 10 became Newport & Sherman's Valley No. 7.

Nos. 11, 12, and 13 were purchased secondhand in 1894 to replace the three engines, 2, 14, and 16, lost in the Overshot and Little Gunpowder Falls trestle accidents in 1891 and 1892. Their origin is not certain, but they are thought to have come from the Addison & North Pennsylvania, which converted to 4'-8½″ in 1893. No. 11 was probably A&NP 6, but possibly 1 (Hinkley #1575, 1882) or 2 (Hinkley #1576, 1882). Nos. 12 and 13 are probably A&NP 3 and 4.

THE BALTIMORE & LEHIGH R. W.
COMPANY.
ONE PASSAGE
BALDWIN
TO
BYNUM

2847

BALTIMORE & LEHIGH RAILROAD—GAUGE 4' - 8½"

Number	Wheel Arrangement	Builder	Builder's Number	Year Built	Drivers	Cylinders	Pressure	Tractive Effort	Total Weight
1.	4-6-0	Richmond	3101	1900	62"	19x24"	180	21,040 lbs.	120,000 lbs.
2.	4-6-0	Richmond	3102	1900	62"	19x24"	180	21,040 lbs.	120,000 lbs.
3.	4-6-0	Richmond	3103	1900	62"	19x24"	180	21,040 lbs.	120,000 lbs.
4.	4-6-0	Richmond	3104	1900	62"	19x24"	180	21,040 lbs.	120,000 lbs.
5.	4-6-0	Richmond	3105	1900	62"	19x24"	180	21,040 lbs.	120,000 lbs.

Notes: Baltimore & Lehigh standard gauge locomotives 1-5 were delivered August 23, 1900, but were found to be too heavy for the railroad. All were returned to the builder and resold, still bearing B&L lettering. Nos. 1-3 were sold February 13, 1901, to the Toledo St. Louis & Western. They were numbered 109-111, class E-2. About 1910 they were reclassified G-6. All three were used in freight service until 1905, but thereafter in passenger operation. In 1924, following absorption of the TStL&W by the Nickel Plate Road, the engines became NKP 809-811, class P-5. They were used in freight service on the Cloverleaf District. The engines were scrapped at Frankfort: 809 in August 1927, 810 in February 1929, and 811 in July 1929.

B&L No. 4 went to the Little Rock & Hot Springs Western as its No. 5. Upon absorption of the LR&HSW by the St. Louis Iron Mountain & Southern, the engine became StLIM&S and Missouri Pacific No. 7601. It was reported active in 1925, but was out of the roster by 1929.

B&L No. 5 was bought by the Shamokin Coal Company of Pennsylvania. It became Mt. Carmel & Natalie No. 5, then Philadelphia & Reading second No. 526 in 1908. It was scrapped in 1922.

Maryland & Pennsylvania Nos. 20, 21 and 22 were originally owned by the Baltimore & Lehigh. See M&PA roster below.

EASTERN DIVISION, PEACH BOTTOM RAILWAY – PEACH BOTTOM RAILROAD – LANCASTER OXFORD & SOUTHERN RAILWAY – GAUGE: 3' - 0"

Number	Wheel Arrangement	Builder	Builder's Number	Year Built	Drivers	Cylinders	Total Weight	Name
1.	2-4-0	Porter-Bell		1873		8x16"		S. R. Dickey
2.	2-4-0	Porter-Bell	224	1875		10x16"	14 tons	Robert Fulton
3.	4-4-0	Pittsburgh	785	1885	43"	12x18"	20 tons	
4.	4-4-0	Mount Savage	36	1883			20 tons	
5.	4-4-0	Baldwin	26002	1905	45"	12x18"	25 tons	
6.	4-4-0	Baldwin	26003	1905	45"	12x18"	25 tons	

Note: No. 4 was purchased from the West Virginia & Pittsburgh in the 1890s.

MARYLAND & PENNSYLVANIA RAILROAD — GAUGE: 4' - 8½"

Number	Wheel Arrangement	Builder	Builder's Number	Year Built	Drivers	Cylinders	Pressure	Tractive Effort	Total Weight	Name
1.	4-4-0	Baldwin	14354	1895	62"	16x24"	160	13,470 lbs.	147,480 lbs.	S. M. Manifold
2.	2-6-0	Baldwin	14408	1895	56"	17x24"	160	16,844 lbs.	159,320 lbs.	J. C. Neville
3.	4-4-0	Baldwin	14547	1895	62"	16x24"	160	13,470 lbs.	147,480 lbs.	W. F. Walworth
4.	4-4-0	Richmond	3287	1901	62"	17x24"	180	16,640 lbs.	183,100 lbs.	
5.	4-4-0	Richmond	3288	1901	62"	17x24"	180	16,640 lbs.	183,100 lbs.	
6.	4-4-0	Richmond	3289	1901	62"	17x24"	180	16,640 lbs.	183,100 lbs.	
20.	0-4-0st	PW&BRR Wilmington shops		1887	50"	15x24"	125	11,475 lbs.	72,000 lbs.	
21.	4-6-0	PRR, Altoona shops	599	1881	50"	18x22"	125	15,150 lbs.	84,800 lbs.	
22.	4-6-0	PRR, Altoona shops	597	1881	50"	18x22"	125	15,150 lbs.	84,800 lbs.	
23.	2-8-0	Baldwin	20003	1902	50"	19x24"	175	25,770 lbs.	212,863 lbs.	
24.	2-8-0	Baldwin	20004	1902	50"	19x24"	175	25,770 lbs.	212,863 lbs.	
25.	2-8-0	Baldwin	25426	1905	50"	19x24"	175	25,770 lbs.	212,863 lbs.	
26.	2-6-0	Baldwin	25694	1905	57"	20x26"	185	28,691 lbs.	273,900 lbs.	
26.	2-8-0	Baldwin	38697	1912	50"	19x24"	175	25,770 lbs.	212,863 lbs.	
27.	4-6-0	Baldwin	29760	1906	56"	19x24"	180	23,660 lbs.	208,633 lbs.	
28.	4-6-0	Baldwin	34995	1910	56"	19x24"	180	23,660 lbs.	208,633 lbs.	
29.	0-6-0	Baldwin	39492	1913	50"	20x26"	180	31,810 lbs.	214,453 lbs.	
30.	0-6-0	Baldwin	40913	1913	50"	20x26"	180	31,810 lbs.	216,453 lbs.	
41.	2-8-0	Baldwin	41504	1914	51"	22x28"	190	43,000 lbs.	316,530 lbs.	
42.	2-8-0	Baldwin	41505	1914	51"	22x28"	190	43,000 lbs.	316,530 lbs.	
43.	2-8-0	Baldwin	58491	1925	51"	22x28"	190	43,000 lbs.	330,850 lbs.	

Diesel-Electric Locomotives

Number	Wheel Arrangement	Builder	Builder's Number	Year Built		
70.	B-B	GM/EMD	4162	1946	600 HP	EMD class SW-1
80.	B-B	GM/EMD	4160	1946	1000 HP	EMD class NW-2
81.	B-B	GM/EMD	4161	1946	1000 HP	EMD class NW-2
82.	B-B	GM/EMD	15558	1951	1200 HP	EMD class SW-9
83.	B-B	GM/EMD	654	1937	900 HP	EMD class SC, modified
84.	B-B	GM/EMD	16330	1952	1200 HP	EMD class SW-9
85.	B-B	GM/EMD	1455	1941	1000 HP	EMD class NW-2
86.	B-B	GM/EMD	18421	1953	1500 HP	EMD class GP-7

Notes: Nos. 1, 2 and 3 were built for the York Southern at the time of its conversion to standard gauge. No. 1 was retired in 1921, No. 2 in 1927, and No. 3 in 1920. Boiler pressure of 2 was reduced to 155 at an unknown date.

No. 4 received electric headlight, 1919; improved headlight, 1934. Retired, 1947.

No. 5 received electric headlight, 1918; improved headlight, 1934; steel cab at unknown date. Abandoned at Baltimore, 1936.

No. 6 received superheater, 1919; electric headlight and automatic drifting valve, 1920; piston valves, 1924; improved headlight, 1934; steel cab at unknown date. Sold for scrap, 1952.

No. 20 was ex-Pennsylvania Railroad A-2 class, No. 1160 or 1161. Sold to Canton RR, 1906. Weights shown for 20-22 are without tender.

No. 21 was ex-Pennsylvania Railroad G-2 class, No. 628. Sold to Canton Railroad, May, 1909.

No. 22 was ex-Pennsylvania Railroad G-2 class, No. 620. Retired, 1914. Became South Florida & Gulf, No. 4.

No. 23 was given southern valve gear, 1915; power reverse, 1917; electric headlight, 1921. Retired, 1947.

No. 24 received steam heat line, southern valve gear and power reverse, 1916; electric headlight, 1920. Retired, 1936.

No. 25 received electric headlight, 1919. Retired, 1939.

First 26 was sold almost immediately upon arrival to the Chicago & Illinois Western, where it became No. 201. It was retired by the C&IW in 1935.

Second 26 received electric headlight, 1919. Retired, 1947.

No. 27 was given a flange oiler, 1916; electric headlight, 1919; superheater and Walschaerts valve gear, 1922. Retired, 1955.

No. 28 was given an electric headlight, 1919; superheater, Walschaerts valve gear and new valves, 1924; improved headlight, 1934. Retired, 1955.

No. 29 received steam heat line, 1916; electric headlight, 1919; power reverse gear, 1934. Retired, 1956.

No. 30 was originally equipped with Walschaerts valve gear; received electric headlight, 1919; Farlow draft gear and strengthened end sills, 1924. Retired, 1956.

No. 41 was originally equipped with Walschaerts valve gear; received electric headlight, 1919; Farlow draft gear and strengthened end sills, 1924; thermic syphons, 1927; power reverse gear, 1934. Retired, 1957.

No. 42 was originally equipped with Walschaerts valve gear; received electric headlight, 1919; Farlow draft gear and strengthened end sills, 1924; power reverse gear, 1926; feedwater heater, 1929. Retired, 1952.

No. 43 was originally equipped with feedwater heater and Walschaerts valve gear; received adjustable driving box wedges, 1929; power reverse gear, 1934. Retired, 1956.

No. 70 was sold in May 1959, to A. J. O'Neill of Lansdowne, Pennsylvania, who sold it to the Republic Steel Company. It operates as No. 326 at the Republic plant at Canton, Ohio.

No. 80 was sold in November 1959, directly to Republic Steel, for whom it operates as No. 334 at the Canton plant.

No. 83 was built as Philadelphia Bethlehem & New England No. 206, class SC, 600 HP; sold January 1947, became Steelton & Highspire No. 23. Rebuilt September 1957 with EMD 8-567C 900 HP engine. Acquired by M&PA December 1967.

No. 84 was built as Pittsburgh & Lake Erie No. 8952, renumbered 1243 c. January 1972. Leased to Montour Railroad as No. 74 in 1974-75. Acquired by M&PA March 1976.

No. 85 was built as Reading No. 92. Acquired by M&PA March 1976.

No. 86 was built as Reading No. 621. Acquired by M&PA March 1976.

EQUIPMENT ROSTER
MARYLAND AND PENNSYLVANIA RAILROAD
Compiled by Charles T. Mahan, Jr.

Coach	Number	Built	Acquired	Disposition and Notes
B&L 1	1	1875	1901	— retired between 1915 and 1919
B&L 2	2	1875	1901	1919 — reblt. to bag.-coach
B&L 3	3	1875	1901	— reblt. to bag.-coach
B&L 4	4		1900	1914 — sold to E. H. Wilson & Co.
B&L 6	6		1900	1915 — sold to E. H. Wilson & Co.
B&L 7	7	1880	1900	1921 — retired, reblt. to camp car 1923
B&L 8	8	1880	1900	1919 — sold to Aransas Harbor Term. Rwy.
B&L 9	9	1880	1900	1914 — retired
B&L 10	10	1880	1900	1914 — sold to E. H. Wilson & Co.
	11	1910	New	1955 — scrapped
	12	1909	"	1941 — sold to U.S. Army (Aberdeen P.G.)
	13	1906	"	1935 — retired
	14	1906	"	1941 — sold to U.S. Army (Aberdeen P.G.)
	15	1902	"	1917 — destroyed on M&PA
	16	1902	"	1937 — conv. to camp car
	17	1902	"	1936 — retired
	18	1902	"	1952 — retired
	19	1911	"	1955 — scrapped
	20	1913	"	1955 — to NRHS, to Strasburg R.R. 1958
	21	1903	1914	1936 — retired, ex. PRR 3050
	22	1903	1914	1926 — reblt. to bag.-coach, ex. PRR 3783
	23	1903	1914	1923 — reblt. to bag.-coach, ex. PRR 2998
	24	1903	1914	1936 — retired, ex. PRR 3792
	25	1903	1914	1923 — reblt. to bag.-coach, ex. PRR 3023
Mail-Coach				
B&L 5	5	1880	1900	1920 — retired, conv. to storeroom at Baltimore
Baggage-Coach				
	2	1875	1901	1923 — retired, reblt. from coach 1919
	3	1875	1901	1923 — retired, reblt. from coach
B&L 20	20		1900	1916 — retired
B&L 21	21	1890	1900	— renumbered 51 about 1914
	22	1903	1914	1939 — retired, reblt. from coach 1926
	23	1903	1914	1926 — retired, reblt. from coach 1923
	25	1903	1914	1938 — retired, reblt. from coach 1923
	51	1890	1900	1919 — sold to Aransas Harbor Term. Rwy.; renumbered from 21 about 1914

Baggage-Mail	Number	Built	Acquired	Disposition and Notes
B&L 30	30	1895	1900	1922 — dest. by fire at Balto. frt. house
B&L 31	31		1900	
B&L 32	32		1900	1907 — scrapped
	33	1908	New	1955 — scrapped
	34	1909	"	1955 — scrapped
	35	1887	1920	1947 — retired, conv. to storeroom at Fallston—reblt. from Colo. Midland baggage No. 306 in 1921
	35	1906	New	1955 — to NRHS, to B&O museum— reblt. from baggage No. 42 in 1942

Baggage				
B&L 40	40		1902	1916 — retired
B&L 41	41		1902	1910 — reblt. to old X3
	42	1906	New	1942 — reblt. to bag.-mail No. 35
	43	1906	"	1920 — dest. in wreck at Woodbrook
	44	1912	"	1955 — scrapped, reblt. in 1934
	45	1887	1920	1938 — retired, ex. Colo. Midland No. 305

Milk-Refrigerator				
	401	1904	1920	1927 — dismantled, ex. Armour Ref. Co. No. 49501, parts used for No. 405
	402	1900	1920	1928 — dismantled, ex. Armour Ref. Co. No. 49416, parts used for No. 406
	405	1927	New	1936 — retired, blt. by M&PA
	406	1928	"	1938 — retired, blt. by M&PA
	420		1927	1929 — returned to Mather Humane Stock Transp. Co. (MRRX 800) from whom car was leased

Caboose				
B&L 1000, M&P 1000	2000	1895		1916 — retired
B&L 419, M&P 1001	2001	1895		1917 — destroyed on M&PA
M&P 1002	2002	1905	New	— blt. by M&PA, side door added 1961
	2003	1901	1917	— ex. Kanawa & Michigan No. 65
	2004	1909	1918	1937 — retired, ex. K&M No. 71
	2005	1889	1925	— ex. Pittsburgh & Lake Erie No. 114
	2006	1910	1937	1959 — sold to Strasburg R.R., No. C2, ex. PRR No. 476582

MARYLAND AND PENNSYLVANIA RAILROAD
Notes on Passenger Equipment

Coaches 11 thru 20 were built by A.C.F., Jackson and Sharp Works, Wilmington, Del.

Data from the order of No. 11 (also 12): length of body 50′0″; width 9′8″; length over platforms 56′4″; Interior paint, green; seat covering, crimson plush; Exterior paint, Tuscan Red; lettering, aluminum; Door locks, to fit PRR key.

Coaches 21 thru 25 were purchased secondhand from E. H. Wilson & Co. in 1914. They were PRR cars, class Pk (one, at least, was not), and 25 had a "Jim Crow" section. Coaches 4, 6 and 10 were given in part payment and possibly went to Canada for work train service.

1st 35 and 45 (ex. Colorado Midland) were purchased from the Arkansas Valley Interurban Railway in 1920. They were built by the Pullman Co. in July 1887.

Baggage-mail cars 33 and 34, and baggage cars 42, 43 and 44 were built in the M&P shops; 33 was rebuilt in 1935; 34 in 1936; 44 was rebuilt in 1934.

Baggage cars 40 and 41 were purchased from E. H. Wilson & Co. and were former Northern Central cars.

Notes on Cabooses

B&L 419 rebuilt from boxcar of same number.

Numbers 1000, 1001, 1002 changed to 2000, 2001, 2002 respectively on Nov. 18, 1911.

2003 thru 2006 were 4-wheel cars.

MOTOR CARS

Number	Builder	Builder's Number	Year	Type	Weight
61(I).	Russell Co.		1922	120 HP gas-mechanical	28,000 lbs.
61(II).	St. Louis Car Co.— Electro-Motive Corp.	200	1927	275 HP gas electric	91,900 lbs.
62.	St. Louis Car Co.— Electro-Motive Corp.	347	1928	440 HP distillate-electric	122,720 lbs.

Note: No. 61(I) was returned to the builder shortly after delivery.
Nos. 61(II) and 62 were retired in 1955.

POPULATIONS OF MAJOR TOWNS
(1960)

Baltimore	936,000
Towson	61,000
Glenarm	140
Long Green	50
Hyde	100
Baldwin	100
Laurel Brook	25
Fallston	100
Bel Air	4,300
Bynum	25
Forest Hill	200
Rocks	150
Street	75
Pylesville	125
Whiteford	120
Cardiff	450
Delta	822
Bryansville	25
Woodbine	60
Bridgeton	25
Muddy Creek Forks	40
Laurel	30
Brogueville	40
Felton	430
Red Lion	5,594
Dallastown	3,615
Yoe	731
York	53,500

Note: Peach Bottom, York County, is no longer in existence. The site of the town is under water as a result of dam construction on the Susquehanna. Population of the town and some of the adjacent rural area in 1900 was 1,188.

Appendix

MODELING THE MA & PA
by John G. Teichmoeller

As a so-called 12 inch = 1 foot scale model railroad, the Maryland and Pennsylvania has been well represented in the model press as well as in production of numerous manufacturers. The following is a compilation of:

a) Several articles on model railroads representing the Ma & Pa

b) Articles covering construction of Ma & Pa equipment and structures

c) Plans of Ma & Pa equipment

d) Ma & Pa rolling stock that has been offered to the modeler.

This survey of articles has been deliberately selective, aimed at only those which do a credible job of representing Ma & Pa equipment, structures or track arrangements.

MODEL RAILROADS BASED ON THE MA & PA

Schafer, Mike (ed.) *More Railroads You Can Model.* "Maryland & Pennsylvania," Milwaukee: Kalmbach Publishing Co., 1978. pp. 60–67.

Presents scenery and track plan emphasizing the Pennsylvania segment of the Ma & Pa.

Sima, Bud. "The Development of the PURR Lines," *Railroad Model Craftsman,* Vol. 47 (October, 1978), pp. 56–63.

Story, track plan, model and prototype photos of a freelance HO model railroad based on the Ma & Pa. This layout expresses its builder's individuality, yet embodies much of the character of the Maryland section of the Ma & Pa from rolling stock to scenery. Focal point of the layout is an exceptionally effective representation of the Baltimore terminal. An earlier version of the track plan appeared in June 1969 *Model Railroader.*

MA & PA CONSTRUCTION ARTICLES

Sima, A. E., Jr. "Building a Locomotive from Wood and Card," *Model Railroader,* Vol. 39, No. 5 (May, 1972), pp. 48–55.

HO construction article of No. 43 2-8-0.

Sima, A. E., Jr. "Ma & Pa Handcar and Tool Shed," *Model Railroader,* Vol. 45, No. 6 (June, 1978), pp. 60, 61.

Construction article with HO drawings and model and prototype photos.

Sima, Bud. "PURR's Ma & Pa Roundhouse," *NMRA Bulletin,* Vol. 45, No. 8 (March, 1980), pp. 7–13.

HO construction article of Baltimore roundhouse with interesting adaptation of a 180° + roundhouse to a limited space.

Mr. Sima continues to publish his model work, and it seems likely that we will see more construction articles by him on Ma & Pa equipment and structures.

PLANS OF MA & PA ROLLING STOCK

Some of these plans appear in this book without dimensions. The page number is indicated in parentheses in the first column. All of the below are from *Mod* *Railroader* magazine with the issue and page numbers noted. All are drawn b J. Harold Geissel. While they were originally published in various scales, rath complete dimensions are given enabling the modeler in any scale to use them wit scale rules. Finally, 0-6-0 No. 30 appears on page 133 of this book but has not bee published to date in *Model Railroader*.

DESCRIPTION	DRAWING SCALE	SOURCE
Motive Power		
Gas-electric No. 62 (inside front cover)	HO (3.5mm = 1′	January, 1966, pp. 36–37
4-4-0 No. 6 (p. 85)	Q (¼″ = 1′)	March, 1965, pp. 34–37
2-8-0 No. 43 (p. 150)	HO	October, 1959, pp. 38, 39
2-8-0 No. 26 (p. 92)	S (3/16″ = 1′)	September, 1952, pp. 42–43 (Also, Wescott, Linn H. [ed.] *Model Railroader Cyclopedia*, Vol. 1 *Steam Locomotives*, p. 56. Milwaukee, Kalmbach Publishing Co., 1960. [HO drawings])
4-6-0 No. 28 (p. 100)	S	October, 1954, pp. 42, 43 (Also *Model Railroader Cyclopedia*, pp. 112, 113. [HO drawings])
Cars		
Wood Gondola No. 620	S	January, 1969, p. 45
Wood Flatcar No. 120	S	February, 1968, p. 34
Wood Boxcar No. 723	Q	May, 1949, p. 43
8 Wheel Caboose No. 2000	HO	December, 1964, p. 48 (Also "Bull Session," *Model Railroader*, February, 1965, p. 62
4 Wheel Caboose No. 2005	HO	January, 1949, p. 29
Coach No. 20	HO	June, 1968, p. 40
Baggage No. 42	HO	September, 1952, p. 44
Baggage-Mail No. 34	HO	September, 1952, p. 44

COMMERCIAL MODELS

Description	Manufacturer/ Distributor	Approximate Introduction Date	Remarks
HO 2-8-0 No. 26	United/Pacific Fast Mail	1956	Brass import
HO 2 coaches & baggage-mail	Gem	1975	3-car set, brass import
HO Gas-electric No. 62	Gem	1975	Brass import
HO 4-4-0 No. 6	Rok Am/Alco Models	1978	Brass import
HO 0-6-0's No. 29 No. 30	Westside Models	1977	Brass import
HO 4-6-0	Olympia/Gem	1962	Brass import
HO Coach & baggage-mail	Westwood Models	1969	Limited edition Wood & plastic craft construction kit
2 HO Coaches	Westwood Models	1971	Same as above, but both coaches are in this kit
HO Caboose 2000	Overland Models	1979	Brass import
HO 4-6-0	The Locomotive Co.	1978	U.S. made metal construction kit
O 2-8-0 No. 26	Iron Horse Models	1978	Brass import
HO 2-8-0 No. 43	United/Pacific Fast Mail	1971	Brass import
HO 2-8-0 No. 26	Akane/International, Akane/Gem, then Akane	1956/1959/ 1960	Brass import

All of these models were limited production items. Importers and manufacturers do reissue items from time to time, particularly in view of the Ma & Pa's popularity. An active collectors' market exists in this equipment, similar to that for coins and stamps, with prices depending on condition and number of units originally produced. Fortunately for the modeler who cannot afford the brass import prices but has average modeling skills, virtually all of the Ma & Pa's rolling stock were fairly standard production items in their era and can be built by relatively simple techniques of modifying other commercial items using readily available metal and plastic fittings.

In addition to these models, the various 4-wheel cabooses of the Ma & Pa have been offered by other companies under their original prototypes. The wooden flatcars, boxcars and gondolas of the Ma & Pa can be modeled by relettering or slightly modifying other items which have been available. And, of course, the modern diesel switchers are standard commercial units which can be altered with easily made details or with the many diesel detail parts now sold.

MARYLAND & PENNSYLVANIA RAILROAD PRESERVED EQUIPMENT
by Charles T. Mahan, Jr.

Number	Type	Location
20	Coach	Strasburg R.R., "Willow Brook"
35	Baggage-mail	B&O R.R. Museum, Baltimore
101	Inspection car	B&O R.R. Museum, Baltimore
122	Flatcar	Strasburg R.R. No. 64
302	Air dump car	Strasburg R.R., not numbered
713	Boxcar	Strasburg R.R. No. 103
723	Boxcar	Strasburg R.R. No. 104
727	Boxcar	Williams Grove (Pa.) Steam Engine Association
2002	Caboose	Private owner, Bruce, Pa.
2003	Caboose	Red Caboose Lodge, Strasburg, Pa.
2005	Caboose	Lincoln Heritage, Inc., Gettysburg, Pa.
2006	Caboose	New Oxford, Pa.

The conductor controlled backing movements down the Dallastown branch from the rear of the trailer. Note his connection to the train air line. *(William M. Moedinger, Jr.)* Below, No. 42 works hard pulling number 31 over the Jail trestle into Towson. *(Charles T. Mahan, Jr.)*

MARYLAND AND PENNSYLVANIA RAILROAD COMPANY

DISPATCHER'S RECORD OF MOVEMENT OF TRAINS

Form 36 Rev.

TIME TABLE No. 5F

Baltimore, Md., SEP 17 1942 .... 194......

RECORD OF WEATHER

	6 A.M.		8 A.M.		10.00 A.M.		12 NOON		4 P.M.		10 P.M.	
	Weather	Temp.	Weather	Temp.	Weather	Temp.	Weather	Temp.	Weather	Temp.	Weather	Temp.
BALTIMORE	Clear N		Clear	74	Cloudy	80	Clear	82	Cldy	84	Clear	74
BEL AIR				70		75		83		84	Rain .17	
DELTA				61		71		81		84	Cldy	78
FELTON				68		74		78		78	Cldy .8	72
YORK												

DISPATCHERS ON DUTY

From 2 o'M. to 6 o'M.
From 6:00 A.M. to 3:00 M.
From 3:00 M. to 7:00 M.
From .... M. to .... M.

SOUTH BOUND

STATIONS	Office Designation	Distance
BALTIMORE	X	
TOWSON	SN	7.0
GLENARM	GN	7.5
FALLSTON	FS	7.8
BEL AIR	KN	4.2

			FR				
3.8	FOREST HILL	FR		927	247	240	
5.0	ROCKS	SO		922	204	219	
7.1	WHITEFORD	WD					
1.4	DELTA	RH			110	12	
12.7	M. C. FORKS	MG		800	752	3	6 Pm
7.1	FELTON	FN			750	253	
4.7	RED LION	RN		748	203	6 232	
2.2	DALLASTOWN	DA		742	700		
9.1	YORK	K			605	6 157 Pm	

WORK TRAINS

Engine No.	Conductor	Time Crew Went On Duty	Time Train Crew Went Off Duty	Engineer	Time Engine Crew Went On Duty	Time Train Crew Went Off Duty	Engineer	Between	and	Time Engine Crew Went On Duty	Commenced Work	Time Engine Crew Went Off Duty	Cleared at

YARD CREWS

Baltimore	27	Cockren					8 45 am	1 00 pm	Wills	8 45 am	1 00 pm		8 30 pm
York	29	McCubbin					7 00 am	1 00 pm	Burt	7 00 am	1 00 pm		12 Noon 4 00 pm
	23	Jacobs					2 00 pm	10 Pm	E.E. Jones	2 00 pm			10 Pm

MEMORANDUM OF EXTRAORDINARY OR UNUSUAL OCCURRENCES:

Train 12 Late 50 Min.

4 Min. Harderman Eng No 7

Glen Arm station was developed as a short-order restaurant. (*Clement D. Erhardt, Jr.*) Forest Hill is preserved as a country store.

Index

Illustrations denoted by*

Mason Locomotive Works, 7*, 11, 205
Missouri Pacific RR, 89, 208
Montour RR, 212
Motor cars, introduction of, 98*, 108-109*, 110-111, 112-113*; last use of, 137, 141, 148*; roster, 109
Mt Carmel & Natalie RR, 208
Mt. Savage shops, 33, 209

N

Nance, J.B., 136, 156
Nance, O.H., 99, 130
Narrow gauge, decision to build, 4, 16; conversion from, 48, 54
Newport & Sherman's Valley RR, 42*, 53*, 207
New York Central RR, 188
Nickel Plate Road, 208
Northern Central Ry., 6, 8, 16, 23, 48, 77, 180, 185, 187

O

Ohio River & Western RR, 60*, 207
Orbisonia, Pa., extension to, 3, 9

P

Panic of 1873, 8-9
Partington, Wm. J., 188, 189
Passenger service: early, 11, 19-20, 24; schedules, 80-81; attrition, 123; end of, 137, 161-162*
Patapsco & Back Rivers RR, 179
Peach Bottom branch: built, 11-12, 14; converted, 51; abandoned, 72; restored, 164, 166*
Peach Bottom RR, 30-31
Peach Bottom Ry., 3-14, 29-31; bankruptcies, 12, 30
Penn Central Tr. Co., 169, 179, 180, 185, 188, 189
Pennsylvania RR, 3, 20, 27, 29, 33, 35, 65, 77, 88, 124, 125, 210, 211; sale of locomotives to B&L, 54, 56*; effort to control York Southern, 48; Frederick branch, 180, 182, 183, 185, 186, 188
Philadelphia, extensions to, 3, 15
Philadelphia & Baltimore Central RR, 15, 38

Philadelphia & Reading RR, 6, 38, 44, 47, 57, 61, 165, 208, 212
Philadelphia, Bethlehem & New England RR, 179, 212
Philadelphia Electric Co., 164, 166, 185
Philadelphia Wilmington & Baltimore RR, 20, 40, 54, 210
Pittsburgh & Lake Erie RR, 212
Pittsburgh Locomotive Works, 13*, 22, 25*, 26*, 36*, 167, 168, 209
Poe, Philip L., 160, 165
Porter-Bell & Co., 7*, 9, 32*, 33, 205, 209

Q

Quarryville: extension to, 33, 35; abandoned, 36

R

Railroad Reorganization & Regulatory Reform Act of 1976, 185
Reading Railway, *see* Philadelphia & Reading
Red Lion: rails reach, 11; traffic, 74, 156, 159, 163, 187; operations at, 96*, 184, 188, 189, 221; embargo beyond, 185, 186
Republic Steel Co., 156-157, 212
Richmond Locomotive Works, 54, 55*, 73*, 80, 208, 209

S

Singerly, extension to, 33
Slate, 3, 16, 91, 114, 159
Slate Ridge & Delta RR, 24
South Buffalo Ry., 179
South Florida & Gulf RR, 211
South Penn Ry., 3, 28
Standard gauge, conversion to, 46, 47-48, 54, 63
Steelton & Highspire RR, 164, 212
Stewartstown RR, 48, 187
Sumter & Choctaw Ry., 165

T

Texas & St. Louis Ry., 43*, 207
Timetables, 5, 31, 94, 149, 199-202
Tionesta Valley RR, 207